High School Spanish Made Simple

Brought to you by

By
Shawn Hays and Amy Dean Beebe

Edited by Amy Dean Beebe and Margaret Mary Wilson, Ed.D

Copyright © 2009 by TutaPoint, LLC
Published by TutaPoint, LLC, publishers Ryan Duques and Michael Callaghan

For information about permission to reproduce or use this book as an instruction aid please contact us at (800) 390-2370, or email us at info@tutapoint.com.
High School Spanish Made Simple, 2009 / 2010 Edition
ISBN: 978-1-934703-46-5
Written by Shawn Hays and Amy Dean Beebe
Edited by Amy Dean Beebe and Margaret Mary Wilson, Ed.D.
Published by TutaPoint, LLC, Ryan Duques and Michael Callaghan Publishers
Design by Elegant D

High School Spanish Made Simple is published by TutaPoint, LLC, a supplemental education company. The publishers have obtained and edited this information and believe that it is accurate and reliable. However, because of possible human or typographical error, the publishers cannot guarantee the accuracy of all examples. Should you find inaccuracies, please email them to info@tutapoint.com

Table of Contents

1.	Capítulo Uno	El Alfabeto – The Alphabet	3
2.	Capítulo Dos	Months, Days and Dates	6
3.	Capítulo Tres	Numbers 0-1,000,000/ Ordinal numbers	11
4.	Capítulo Cuatro	Definite and Indefinite Articles/Spanish Contractions	15
5.	Capítulo Cinco	Adjectives/Nouns and Agreement	21
6.	Capítulo Seis	Demonstratives/Possessives	30
7.	Capítulo Siete	"Who, What, When, Where, Why, How"	39
8.	Capítulo Ocho	Subject Pronouns	42
9.	Capítulo Nueve	Regular Verbs	45
10.	Cápitulo Diez	Ser vs. Estar	53
11.	Capítulo Once	Stem-changing Verbs & Verbs With Irregular "Yo" Forms	57
12.	Capítulo Doce	Direct and Indirect Objects and the Personal "a"	63
13.	Capítulo Trece	Gustar and Gustar-like Verbs	70
14.	Capítulo Catorce	Reflexive Verbs	76
15.	Capítulo Quince	Saber vs Conocer/Pedir vs Preguntar	78
16.	Capítulo Dieciséis	Gerunds/Progressive or "ing" tenses	81
17.	Capítulo Diecisiete	Pretérito/Imperfecto	84
18.	Capítulo Dieciocho	Future and Conditional Tenses	95
19.	Capítulo Diecinueve	The Perfect Tenses: Present and Past	102
20.	Capítulo Veinte	Commands and Subjunctive	111
21.	Capítulo Veintiuno	Por vs Para	125
22.	Capítulo Veintidós	Telling Time	129
23.	Capítulo Veintitrés	Weather	133
24.	Capítulo Veinticuatro	Tener Expressions	135
25.	Capítulo Veinticinco	Useful Spanish Conversation Words/Phrases	139

ANSWER KEYS FOR EACH "PRÁCTICA" 142

CAPÍTULO UNO:
THE SPANISH ALPHABET AND PRONUNCIATION

a = a
b = be
c = ce
d = de
e = e
f = efe
g = ge
h = hache
i = i
j = jota
k = ka
l = ele
m = eme
n = ene
ñ = en-ye
o = o
p = pe
q = cu
r = ere
s = ese
t = te
u = u
v = ve
w = doble ve (or doble u)
x = equis
y = i griega
z = zeta

Spanish is a phonetic language. This means that the words are spelled as they are pronounced. Once you learn the rules, you can go off and pronounce any new Spanish word that you come across!

Las Vocales (The Vowels):

A = "ah" (Ej: agosto, martes)

E = "eh" (Ej. español, tres)

I (Y) = "eee"   (Ej. invierno, diciembre)

O = "oh"   (Ej. otoño, cómico)

U = "oo"   (Ej. uno, lunes)

Los Consonantes (The consonants)
Most of the Spanish consonants are pronounced like or almost like corresponding English consonants. The following, however, deserve special attention:

C is soft when in front of an "e" or "i" (ej. cero, ciento)
  is hard when in front of an "a", "o" or "u" (ej. Carlos, cómico, cuatro)
G is soft when in front of an "e" or "i" (ej. geografía, gimnasio)
  is hard when in front of an "a", "o" or "u" (ej. gato, gordo, guitarra)

H is ALWAYS silent (ej. Hola, hasta pronto)

J is always pronounced like the English "h" (ej. junio, julio, jueves)

LL is pronounced like the English "y" (ej. Me Llamo, llueve)

Ñ sounds like the "ny" combination of the English word "canyon" (ej. mañana)

QU sounds like "k" (ej. qué, quince)

R is a slight tap on the roof of your mouth (ej. pero, enero)

RR (and when R is the first letter of a word) is pronounced with a strong trill (ej. guitarra, carro, Ramón, rápido)

V is pronounced just like a "b"

Z is pronounced like an "s" (ej. diez, zapato)

THE STRESS IN SPANISH WORDS

In Spanish, there are 3 simple rules to help you figure out which syllable is stressed in a word.

Rule #1: If a word ends in a vowel, "n" or "s", the next to the last syllable is stressed. (hola, lunes, señora, septiembre)

Rule #2: If a word ends in any consonant except "n" or "s", the last syllable is stressed. (señor, por favor, usted, hablar)

Rule #3: If a word does not follow Rule #1 or #2, an accent mark shows which syllable is stressed. (ej. miércoles, sábado, estás)

PRÁCTICA
Say and then spell the following words en español:
(ejemplo: Bien/ Be-i-e-ene)

1. Gusto

2. Once

3. Regular

4. Brazo

5. Burro

6. jueves

7. veinte y cinco

8. charlar

9. Geo Fredo

10. matemáticas

CAPÍTULO DOS:
MONTHS, DAYS AND DATES

In Spanish-speaking countries, the week begins on Monday.

lunes
Monday
martes
Tuesday
miércoles
Wednesday
jueves
Thursday
viernes
Friday
sábado
Saturday
domingo
Sunday

Notice that the days of the week are not capitalized.

The days of the week are masculine. (There'll be more on masculine/feminine in Capítulo 4.)

When used with the days of the week, the definite article means "on", not "the".

No trabajo el lunes.
I don't work on Monday.
No trabajo los martes.
I don't work on Tuesdays.
Hay una fiesta el miércoles.
There is a party on Wednesday.
Hay muchas fiestas los viernes.
There are many parties on Fridays.

Days of the week ending in -s do not change form in the plural ... only the article changes.

el lunes
los lunes
el martes
los martes
el miércoles
los miércoles
el jueves
los jueves

el viernes
los viernes
el sábado
los sábados
el domingo
los domingos

Use the verb "ser" to express the day. You will soon learn more about this verb. For now, simply know that the word "es" is a conjugation of this verb, and is the correct verb to use in this case.

¿Qué día es hoy?
What day is today?
Hoy es lunes.
Today is Monday.
Mañana es martes.
Tomorrow is Tuesday.

Notice that the following actions do not occur in the present, but rather in the near future.

Salimos el lunes.
We leave on Monday.
Mañana es domingo.
Tomorrow is Sunday.

Here are the months in Spanish. Note that, like the days of the week, they are not capitalized.

enero
    January
febrero
    February
marzo
    March
abril
    April
mayo
    May
junio
    June
julio
    July
agosto
    August
septiembre
    September
octubre

October
noviembre
November
diciembre
December

To express "in a certain month," use the preposition **en**, which means "in".

Vamos a México **en** enero.
We are going to Mexico in January.

Las clases empiezan **en** el mes de septiembre.
Classes begin in the month of September.

Here are some ways to inquire as to the date.

¿Cuál es la fecha de hoy?
¿A cuántos estamos hoy?
¿Qué día es hoy?
¿A cuántos estamos?

If you are talking about the first day of the month, use the expression "el primer día" or simply "el primero."
¿Qué día es hoy?
Hoy es lunes, el primer día de mayo.
Hoy es lunes, el primero de mayo.
Today is Monday, May 1.

For all other days of the month, use the cardinal numbers.
¿Cuál es la fecha de hoy? (Tuesday, March 25)
Hoy es martes, el veinticinco de marzo.
¿A cuántos estamos hoy? (Sunday, June 3)
Estamos al domingo, el tres de junio.

The Spanish way is to write the day + month + year. This is different from the American way (month + day + year).
el 29 de febrero de 1996
February 29, 1996
29.2.96
2/29/96

PRÁCTICA
Choose the correct translation.

1. Monday
el lunes
El Lunes

2. Tuesday
el martes
El Martes

3. Wednesday
el miércoles
El Miércoles

4. Thursday
el jueves
El Jueves

5. Wednesday
el miércoles
la miércoles

6. Thursday
el jueves
la jueves

7. Friday
el viernes
la viernes

8. Saturday
el sábado
la sábado

9. Sunday
el domingo
la domingo

Supply the correct day of the week.

10. Hoy es lunes. Mañana es _____. (Today is …, tomorrow is …)

11. Hoy es martes. Mañana es _____.

12. Hoy es miércoles. Mañana es _____.

13. Hoy es jueves. Mañana es _____.

14. Hoy es viernes. Mañana es _____.

15. Hoy es sábado. Mañana es _____.

16. Hoy es domingo. Mañana es _____.

17. Write the month that comes next.
1. enero, febrero,
2. marzo, abril,
3. mayo, junio,
4. julio, agosto,
5. septiembre, octubre,
6. noviembre, diciembre,

Complete each sentence.

18. ¿Qué fecha es hoy? (April 1)
Hoy es el _____ día de abril.

19. ¿Cuál es la fecha de hoy? (Wednesday, June 20)
Hoy es miércoles, el veinte de_____ .

20. ¿Qué día es hoy? (May 5)
Hoy es el _____ de mayo.

CAPÍTULO TRES: NUMBERS 0-1.000.000

Cardinal numbers (cardinales) are the numbers used for counting; of course they look the same in Spanish as well as in English:

Spanish Numbers	
0 cero	10 diez
1 uno/a	11 once
2 dos	12 doce
3 tres	13 trece
4 cuatro	14 catorce
5 cinco	15 quince
6 seis	16 dieciséis
7 siete	17 diecisiete
8 ocho	18 dieciocho
9 nueve	19 diecinueve

In Spanish uno becomes un when used in front of a masculine noun: un perro, veintiún perros. To refer to a feminine noun una is used: una mujer, treinta y una mujeres. Uno is used only when counting (uno, dos, tres) or for numerals refering to a masculine noun but does not precede that noun: ¿Cuántos hijos tienes? - Uno (or else we simply write) - un hijo

20 veinte
21 veintiuno/a
22 veintidós
21-29 are usually a single word composed as follows: **omit** the last e from veint<u>e</u> and add *i* instead then add the digit = veintiuno, the rest 30-99 can be formed up to three words: treinta y uno.
30 treinta
31 treinta y uno

More Cardinal Numbers	
40 cuarenta	400 cuatrocientos/as
50 cincuenta	500 quinientos/as
60 sesenta	600 seiscientos/as
70 setenta	700 setecientos/as
80 ochenta	800 ochocientos/as
90 noventa	900 novecientos/as
100 cien(to)	1.000 mil
101 ciento uno	1.500 mil quinientos
200 doscientos/as	2.000 dos mil
300 trescientos/as	1.000.000 un millón

So in short, uno in compound numbers loses the -o before masculine nouns, whether singular or plural: cuarenta y un días (forty-one days).

Dates (months and years) are cardinal numbers in Spanish, except for the first of the month: El 8 (ocho) de mayo de 1987 (mil novecientos ochenta y siete) (the eighth of May, 1987). But: Hoy es el primero de enero (Today is January 1st).

Ordinal Numbers
Here are the ordinal numbers first - tenth:

primero
first

segundo
second

tercero
third

cuarto
fourth

quinto
fifth

sexto
sixth

séptimo
seventh

octavo
eighth

noveno
ninth

décimo
tenth

Like most other adjectives, the ordinal numbers have a masculine and a feminine form.

primero
primera
segundo
segunda
tercero
tercera

cuarto
cuarta
quinto
quinta
sexto
sexta
séptimo
séptima
octavo
octava
noveno
novena
décimo
decimal

Like most other adjectives, they also have a singular and plural form.

primero
primeros
segundo
segundos
tercero
terceros
cuarto
cuartos
quinto
quintos
sexto
sextos
séptimo
séptimos
octavo
octavos
noveno
novenos
décimo
décimos

So, the ordinal numbers have four forms, just like other adjectives that end in -o.
primero
primeros
primera
primeras

Primero and tercero drop the -o in the masculine singular adjective form.
el **primer** día
el **tercer** año

Ordinal numbers usually **precede** the noun. However, if the noun they refer to is royalty, a pope, or a street, they come **after** the noun.

Carlos Quinto
("Quinto" comes after "Carlos" - royalty)
el quinto libro
("quinto" comes before "libro")
la Calle Sexta
("sexta" comes after "calle" - street)
la sexta pluma
("sexta" comes before "pluma")
Ordinal numbers are not normally used after 10.
la Calle Dieciséis
Sixteenth Street
el siglo diecinueve
the nineteenth century

CAPÍTULO CUATRO:
DEFINITE & INDEFINITE ARTICLES
SPANISH CONTRACTIONS

Definite Articles

The definite articles mean "the" in English, and refer to specific nouns. There are 4 definite articles in Spanish, and which one you use depends on the gender (masculine or feminine) and number (singular or plural) of the noun it refers to. Masculine nouns use **el or los**; feminine nouns use **la or las**. All nouns in Spanish are either masculine or feminine. For example, even though a book isn't a boy, it is a masculine word and its gender must be memorized (el libro).

MASCULINE EL (singular) LOS (plural)	THE
FEMININE LA (singular) LAS (plural)	THE

Ejemplos

Masculine	Feminine
El libro- the book	La mochila- the backpack
El cuaderno- the notebook	La bandera- the flag
El papel- the paper	La pizarra- the chalkboard
El borrador- the eraser	La mesa- the table
El reloj- the clock	La silla- the chair
Los libros- the books	Las carpetas- the folders
Los papeles- the papers	Las clases- the classes
Los borradores- the erasers	Las puertas- the doors
Los escritorios- the desks	Las banderas- the flags

INDEFINITE ARTICLES

The indefinite articles, **a, an or some** in English are used to refer to non-specific things. The equivalent depends on whether the noun it refers to is masculine or feminine, or singular or plural. Here are the the indefinite articles:

MASCULINE UN-singular	A,AN
UNOS- plural	SOME
FEMININE UNA-singular	A,AN
UNAS-plural	SOME

Ejemplos

Masculine	Feminine
Un libro- A book	Una mochila- a backpack
Un cuaderno-a notebook	Una carpeta- a folder
Un lápiz- a pencil	Una clase- a class
Un papel- a paper	Una silla- a chair
Unos libros-some books	Unas sillas- some chairs
Unos escritorios- some desks	Unas mochilas- some backpacks
Unos cuadernos- some notebooks	Unas mesas- some tables

PRÁCTICA

Circle the correct answer.

1. the books
A. el libro
B. la revista
C. los libros
D. las revistas

2. an airplane
A. un avión
B. una avión
C. unos aviones
D. unas muchachas

3. some pencils
A. un lápiz
B. una actriz
C. unos lápices
D. unas actrices

4. the (female) professor
A. el profesor
B. la profesora
C. un profesor
D. una profesora

5. a decision
A. la decisión
B. unas decisiones
C. un idioma
D. una decisión

6. a (male) cat
A. los gatos
B. un gato
C. el gato
D. la gata

7. the voice
A. una voz
B. la voz
C. la conversación
D. las conversaciones

8. some students (male and female)
A. unas estudiantes
B. los estudiantes
C. unos estudiantes
D. el estudiante

True or false?
9. There are only two definite articles: el and la.
true
false

10. There are four definite articles: el, la, los, las.
true
false

11. There are only two indefinite articles: un and una.
true
false

12. There are four indefinite articles: un, una, unos, unas.
true
false

13. Un means "a, an" when used before a masculine noun.
true
false

14. When referring to a specific noun, use the indefinite articles.
true
false

15. Una means "a, an" when used before a feminine noun.
true
false

16. You choose the form of the article by whether or not the noun it introduces is masculine or feminine, singular or plural.
true
false

Choose the appropriate article.
17. (some chairs)
_____ sillas
18. (a table)
_____ mesa
19. (a cat)
_____ gata
20. (some books)
_____ libros

Contractions
When **a** or **de** precedes the definite article **el**, the two words combine to form a contraction. That is, two words become one. These are **always** contracted in Spanish.

a + el = al   de + el = del

Incorrect:
¿Llevas a el hermano de Raúl?
Correct:

¿Llevas al hermano de Raúl?
Incorrect:
¿El libro es de el profesor?
Correct:
¿El libro es del profesor?

De + la, de + las, de + los, a + la, a + las, and a + los are **never** contracted.
¿Llevas al hermano de Raúl?
Are you taking Raul's brother?
No, llevo a las hermanas de Pilar.
No, I'm taking Pilar's sisters.
¿El libro es del profesor?
Is the book the profesor's?
No, el libro es de la profesora.
No, the book is the profesor's (fem).

Be careful with "el" and "él". The pronoun (él) does have a written accent and means "he." The definite article (el) does not have a written accent and means "the."

el libro / the book
él come / he eats

Only the definite article (el) is contracted. The pronoun (él) is not.
La Casa Blanca es la casa del presidente.
The White House is the president's house.
Es la casa de él.
It's his house.
A él no le gusta fumar.
He doesn't like to smoke.

PRÁCTICA

Fill in the blanks with the correct contraction

1. Vengo_____ fiesta de la universidad.
(I come to the college party.)

2. ¿A qué hora llamas _____ profesora?
(At what time do you call the teacher?)

3. Le llamo_____ mediodía.
(I call her at noon.)

4. ¿Los libros son_____ Señor Rodríguez?
(Are the books Mr. Rodriguez's?)

5. No, son_____ Señora García.
(No, they are Mr. Garcia's.)

6. ¿Tienes que ir_____ casa de tu amigo?
(Do you have to go to your friend's house?)

7. No, tengo que ir_____ laboratorio para estudiar.
(No, I have to go to the lab to study.)

8. ¿Adónde llevas_____ chicas?
(To where are you bringing the girls?)

9. Llevo a las chicas_____ apartamento.
(I'm bringing the girls to the apartment.)

10. ¿De quién son las plumas? Son_____ profesora.
(Who's are the pens? They are the teacher's.)

CAPÍTULO CINCO:
ADJECTIVES/NOUNS

Adjectives

In Spanish, adjectives have to agree in number and gender with the nouns they accompany. In English there is nothing comparable to this. In most cases, contrary to English usage, adjectives follow their nouns. The masculine form of the adjective ends in –o and the feminine form end in –a, and the plurals are –os and –as respectively:

Examples:

El hijo- the son

La hija- the daughter

el señor simpático- the charming gentleman

la señora simpática- the charming lady

los señores simpáticos- the charming gentlemen

las señoras simpáticas- the charming ladies

What would be the correct letter to put on the end of these adjectives?

Masculine	Feminine
Buen_	Buen_
Atrevid__	Atrevid__
Seri__	Seri__
Talentos__	Talentos__
Alt__	Alt__

If the masculine singular of the adjective ends in an –e, the feminine singular is the same as the masculine.
Ejemplos:
Un país importante- an important country

Una familia importante- an important family

Países important**es**- important countries

Familias important**es**- important families

If the masculine adjectival form ends in a consonant, there is no change for the feminine singular, and we form the plurals of both genders by adding –es.

Ejemplos

Un juego difícil- a difficult game

Una lengua difícil- a difficult language

Jueg**os** difícil**es**- difficult games

Lengu**as** difícil**es**- difficult languages

Nouns

Although Spanish nouns are classified as either feminine or masculine, remember that there can be feminine nouns that describe things we think of as masculine, and vice versa. For example, *un elefante*, which is masculine in form, refers to an elephant whether it's male or female. Also, *una persona* means "a person" even if it's a male. For some people, it might be easier to think of them as simply two classifications rather than giving them a sexual identity.

The basic rule is that masculine nouns go with masculine adjectives and articles, and feminine nouns go with feminine adjectives and articles. In English, the articles are "a," "an" and "the." Also note that in Spanish many adjectives don't have separate masculine and feminine forms. If you use a pronoun to refer to a masculine noun, you use a masculine pronoun; feminine pronouns refer to feminine nouns.

Nouns and adjectives that end in -o (or -os for plural adjectives) generally are masculine, and nouns and adjectives that end in -a (or -as for plural adjectives) generally are feminine, although there are exceptions. For example, *cada día* means "each day." *Día* ("day") is a masculine noun; *cada* ("each") can be either feminine or masculine.

Since you can't always tell by looking at a noun or knowing its meaning whether it's masculine or feminine, most dictionaries use notations (*f* or *m*) to indicate the gender. And it's also common in vocabulary lists, such as many of them at, to precede words with an *el* for masculine words and a *la* for feminine words. (*El* and *la* both mean "the.")

Here are examples that show some of the ways a noun's gender affects the usage of other words. Some of the examples may be more understandable once you study the lessons on adjectives, articles and pronouns.

- **the** man: **el** *hombre* (masculine article, masculine noun)
- **the** woman: **la** *mujer* (feminine article, feminine noun)
- **a** man: **un** *hombre* (masculine article, masculine noun)
- **a** woman: **una** *mujer* (feminine article, feminine noun)
- **the** men: **los** *hombres* (masculine article, masculine noun)
- **the** women: **las** *mujeres* (feminine article, feminine noun)
- the **fat** man: *el hombre **gordo*** (masculine adjective, masculine noun)
- the **fat** woman: *la mujer **gorda*** (feminine adjective, feminine noun)
- **some** men: **unos** *hombres* (masculine determiner, masculine noun)
- **some** women: **unas** *mujeres* (feminine determiner, feminine noun)
- He is fat: *Él es **gordo***. (masculine pronoun, masculine adjective)
- She is fat: *Ella es **gorda***. (feminine pronoun, feminine adjective)

If you have two or more nouns that are being described by a single adjective, and they are of mixed genders, the masculine adjective is used.

Example: *El **carro** es **caro***, the car is expensive (masculine noun and adjective). *La **bicicleta** es **cara***, the bicycle is expensive (feminine noun and adjective). *El **carro** y la **bicicleta** son **caros***, the car and the bicycle are expensive (masculine and feminine nouns described by a masculine adjective).

Plural forms of nouns

If a noun ends in a vowel, make it plural by adding -s.

libro: libros

(libro + s)

pluma: plumas

(pluma + s)

chico: chicos

(chico + s)

señora: señoras

(señora + s)

The definite articles (el, la) also change in the plural form. They become "los" and "las."

el libro: **los libros**

la pluma: **las plumas**

el chico: **los chicos**

la señora: **las señoras**

If a noun ends in a consonant, make it plural by adding -es.

el borrador: los borradores

(borrador + es)

la universidad: las universidades

(universidad + es)

el profesor: los profesores

(profesor + es)

la ciudad: las ciudades

(ciudad + es)

If a noun ends in -ión, add -es and drop the written accent.

el avión: **los aviones**

la conversación: **las conversaciones**

la sección: **las secciones**

la televisión: **las televisiones**

Note: You may wonder why "avión" isn't feminine. Notice that it doesn't qualify for our rule which says that all nouns ending in **-ción** and **sión** are feminine.

If a noun ends in -z, add -es and change the z to c.

el lápiz: **los lápices**

la voz: **las voces**

el tapiz: **los tapices**

la actriz: **las actrices**

When the plural refers to two or more nouns of different genders, the masculine plural is used.

2 perros + 6 perras = 8 perros (not perr**a**s)
1 gato + 8 gatas = 9 gatos (not gat**a**s)

A few nouns are "compound nouns," that is, they are formed by combining two words into one.

(Example: abre + latas = abrelatas / open + cans = can opener)

These compound nouns are always masculine, and the plural is formed by changing the "el" to "los."

el abrelatas
los abrelatas

el paraguas (the umbrella)
los paraguas

Let's review the rules for making nouns plural.

- If a noun ends in a vowel, simply add -s.
- If a noun ends in a consonant, simply add -es.
- If a noun ends in a -z, change the z to c before adding -es.
- If a noun ends in **ión**, drop the written accent before adding -es.

- If the plural refers to a mixed group, use the masculine.
- For compound nouns, change "el" to "los"

PRÁCTICA

1. Which word is masculine?

la casa
la mesa
el libro
la ventana

2. Which word is feminine?

el chico
el hermano
el abuelo
la hermana

3. Which word is masculine?

el cuaderno
la pluma
la maestra
la profesora

4. Which word is feminine?

el número
el teléfono
el muchacho
la tía

5. ¿Cuál es la palabra masculina?

la mañana
la palabra
el diccionario
la tarea

Choose between masculine or feminine.

6. el libro

is a masculine word
is a feminine word

7. la pluma

is a masculine word
is a feminine word

8. el cuaderno

is a masculine word
is a feminine word

9. el escritorio

is a masculine word
es una palabra femenina

10. la acción

es una palabra masculina
es una palabra femenina

Fill in with the correct letter.

11. el libr__

12. la mes__

13. el gat__

14. la gat__

15. el chic__

16. la chic__

17. el cuadern __

18. la plum__

19. el vestid __

20. la corbat __

PRÁCTICA

Choose the correct plural form.

1. el libro

los libroes
los libros

2. el lápiz

los lápices
los lápizes

3. la universidad

las universidads
las universidades

4. la secretaria

la secretarias
las secretarias

5. el mapa

el mapas
los mapas

6. la conversación

las conversaciones
las conversaciónes

True or false?

8. If a noun ends in -o, make it plural by adding -s.

true
false

9. If a noun ends in -ión, make it plural by simply adding -es.

true
false

10. If a noun ends in -a, make it plural by adding -s.

true

false

11. If a noun ends in -ión, make it plural by adding -es and dropping the written accent.

true
false

12. To form the plural of nouns that end in a vowel, add -s.

true
false

13. If a noun ends in a consonant, make it plural by adding -es.

true
false

14. If a noun ends in -z, make it plural by changing the z to c, and adding -es.

true
false

Complete with the missing letters to correctly form the plural.

15. los av_____ (el avión)

16. los lápi_____ (el lápiz)

17. las profesor_____ (la profesora)

18. los profesor_____ (el profesor)

19. las universidad_____ (la universidad)

20. los planeta_____ (el planeta)

CAPÍTULO SEIS: DEMONSTRATIVES/POSSESSIVES

There are two types of demonstratives: demonstrative adjectives and demonstrative pronouns. The first step in clearly understanding these two topics is to review the differences between "adjectives" and "pronouns."

adjective
describes a noun

pronoun
takes the place of a noun

In the following sentences, the words in **bold** all function as adjectives, since they all describe the noun "book."

Give me the **red** book.
Give me the **big** book.
Give me **that** book.
Give me **this** book.

Notice that adjectives answer the question "Which?" in relation to the nouns that they modify. (Which book? The *red* book. The *big* book. *That* book. *This* book.)

In the following sentences, the words in **bold** all function as pronouns, since they all take the place of a noun.

Maria is next; give **her** the ball.
Juan is here; say hello to **him**.
That pencil is yours; **this** is mine.
This book is mine; **that** is yours.

Notice that pronouns replace a noun. ("her" replaces "Maria" - "him" replaces "Juan" - "this" replaces "pencil" - "that" replaces "book")

As you have just seen, the words "this" and "that" can function as both adjectives and pronouns.

This book is mine. (adjective)
This (one) is mine. (pronoun)

That book is yours. (adjective)
That (one) is yours. (pronoun)

The same is true in Spanish.

Juan reads **this** book. (adjective)
Juan lee **este** libro.

Juan reads **this**. (pronoun)

Juan lee **este**.

That statue is Greek.
Esa estatua es griega.

That (one) is American.
Esa es americana.

Spanish has three words where English only has two. In English, we say "this" or "that" depending upon whether the object is close to us or not. In Spanish, we also say "this" and "that," but there is another, separate word used to mean "that one over there." This form is used when the object is more than just a short distance away, for example, on the other side of the room. Here are the three forms for "this" "that" and "that one over there."

este
this

ese
that

aquel
that one over there

Remember that in Spanish, adjectives have four forms: masculine singular, masculine plural, feminine singular, feminine plural. For example the adjective "short" has four forms in Spanish: bajo, bajos, baja, bajas.

el chico **bajo**
los chicos **bajos**

la chica **baja**
las chicas **bajas**

The demonstrative adjectives also have four forms:

este libro (this book)
estos libros (these books)
esta pluma (this pen)
estas plumas (these pens)

ese libro (that book)
esos libros (those books)
esa pluma (that pen)
esas plumas (those pens)

aquel libro (that book over there)
aquellos libros (those books over there)
aquella pluma (that pen over there)
aquellas plumas (those pens over there)

Here are the corresponding demonstrative pronouns:

este (this one - masculine)
estos (these ones - masculine)
esta (this one - feminine)
estas (these ones - feminine)

ese (that one - masculine)
esos (those ones - masculine)
esa (that one - feminine)
esas (those ones - feminine)

aquel (that one over there - masc.)
aquellos (those ones over there - masc.)
aquella (that one over there - fem.)
aquellas (those ones over there - fem.)

Each demonstrative pronoun also has a neuter form. They do not change for number or gender, and they are used to refer to abstract ideas, or to an unknown object.

esto (this matter, this thing)
eso (that matter, that thing)
aquello (that matter/thing over there)

PRÁCTICA

Match in gender and number using *the Spanish form of* **THIS**.

1. Yo prefiero _____ manzana verde. (I prefer this green apple.)

2. _____ zanahorias son muy bonitas. (These carrots are very pretty.)

3. _____ pescado no me parece bueno. (This fish seems fine to me.)

4. ¿Buscas _____ gambas frescas? (Are you looking for this fresh shrimp?)

5. No me gustan _____ plátanos. (I don't like these bananas.)

6. A Juan le gusta mucho _____ torta de chocolate. (John likes this chocolate cake a lot.)

CAPÍTULO SEIS 33

Now fill in using **that or those**

1. ¿No te gustan _____ ensalada de frutas? (Don't you like that fruit salads?)

2. Yo prefiero _____ fresas frescas. (I prefer those fresh strawberries.)

3. _____ melones son muy dulces. (Those melons are very sweet.)

4. No me gusta _____ ensalada rusa. (I don't like that Russian salad.)

5. Voy a comprar _____ tomates. (I'm going to buy those tomatoes.)

6. Tienes que comer en _____ restaurante. (You have to eat in that restaurant.)

Use **THAT, THOSE** OVER THERE!!!

1. ¿Son _____ galletas de piña? (Are those cookies pineapple?)

2. _____ hombre pide sopa de pollo. (That man asks for chicken soup.)

3. ¿Cuestan mucho _____ pepinos? (Do those cucumbers cost a lot?)

4. Este plato es de Carmen y _____ es de Mario. (This plate is Carmen's and that is Mario's.)

Now MIX them all up!

1. _____ (this) pescado está rico pero _____ (that-near) pescado está malo.

2. No me gustan _____ (these) tomates verdes. Prefiero _____ (those-far) tomates rojos.

3. _____ (those-near) piñas no son dulces. .

4. ¿Quieres comprar _____ (these) uvas?

5. Voy a comprar _____ (those - far) naranjas.

6. Prefieres _____ (this) langosta o _____ (that one -near)?

Possessives

We begin this lesson with a review of the difference between an adjective and a pronoun.

adjective
describes a noun

pronoun
takes the place of a noun

Look at the following sentence pairs. One has an adjective, while the other has a pronoun.

My book is large. (adjective, describes book)
Yours is small. (pronoun, takes the place of noun)

Your car is green. (adjective, describes car)
Mine is red. (pronoun, takes the place of noun)

Now, let's look at each sentence a little more closely.

My book is large.

My is an adjective because it modifies, or describes the noun "book." Furthermore, it is a "possessive" adjective because it tells who owns, or possesses, the book.

Yours is small.

Yours is a pronoun, because it replaces or takes the place of a noun. In this case, the previous sentence tells us that "yours" is replacing the noun "book." Furthermore, it is a "possessive" pronoun because it tells who owns, or possesses, the noun it is replacing.

Your car is green.

Your is an adjective because it modifies the noun "car." Furthermore, it is a "possessive" adjective because it tells who owns, or possesses, the car.

Mine is red.

Mine is a pronoun, because it replaces or takes the place of a noun. In this case, the previous sentence tells us that "mine" is replacing the noun "car." Furthermore, it is a "possessive" pronoun because it tells who owns, or possesses, the noun it is replacing.

So far, we have been talking about the difference between the possessive adjective and the possessive pronoun. You will recall that in a previous lesson, you already learned about the possessive adjectives.

mi(s)
my
mi libro
mis plumas

tu(s)
your (fam. sing.)
tu libro
tus plumas

su(s)
his, her, your (formal), their
su libro
sus plumas

nuestro(-a, -os, -as)
our
nuestro libro
nuestras plumas

vuestro(-a, -os, -as)
your (fam. pl.)
vuestro libro
vuestras plumas

The possessive pronouns are similar to the possessive adjectives, but they are normally used with the definite article.

mine
el mío / la mía
los míos / las mías

yours (familiar)
el tuyo / la tuya
los tuyos / las tuyas

yours (formal), his, hers
el suyo / la suya
los suyos / las suyas

ours
el nuestro / la nuestra
los nuestros / las nuestras

yours (familiar)
el vuestro / la vuestra
los vuestros / las vuestras

yours (formal), theirs
el suyo / la suya
los suyos / las suyas

Now let's translate our model sentences:

Mi libro es grande.
My book is large.

El tuyo es pequeño.
Yours is small.

Tu carro es verde.
Your car is green.

El mío es rojo.
Mine is red.

The previous translations assume that you are talking to a friend, or someone you know well, and are using the informal "tú" form of speech. But remember, Spanish also has a more formal form of speech. The same sentences change if we assume that you are talking to someone in a position of authority, using the more formal "usted" form of speech.

Mi libro es grande. (no change)
My book is large.

El suyo es pequeño. (formal)
Yours (formal) is small.

Su carro es verde. (formal)
Your (formal) car is green.

El mío es rojo. (no change)
Mine is red.

The definite article is usually omitted when the possessive pronoun comes after the verb ser:

El carro grande es mío.
The big car is mine.

El carro pequeño es suyo.
The small car is hers.

Notice the following ambiguity:

El carro grande es suyo.

The big car is his.

El carro grande es suyo.
The big car is hers.

El suyo, la suya, los suyos, las suyas can be clarified as follows:

El carro grande es suyo.
The big car is his. (unclarified)

El carro grande es de él.
The big car is his. (clarified)

La casa pequeña es suya.
The small house is hers. (unclarified)

La casa pequeña es de ella.
The small house is hers. (clarified)

Los carros grandes son suyos.
The big cars are theirs. (unclarified)

Los carros grandes son de ellas.
The big cars are theirs. (clarified)

Las casas pequeñas son suyas.
The small houses are theirs. (unclarified)

Las casas pequeñas son de ellos.
The small houses are theirs. (clarified)

Note: de + el are contracted to form "del," however, de + él are **not** contracted.

PRÁCTICA

Translate the following phrases into Spanish

1. Your friends (you formal)
2. His house
3. Our shoes
4. Their restaurant
5. Your sisters (you all familiar)
6. My juice
7. Your backpack (you familiar)
8. Her cake
9. Its nose
10. Your books and pens (you all formal)

CAPÍTULO SIETE:

"WHO, WHAT, WHEN, WHERE, WHY, HOW..." QUESTIONS (INTERROGATIVAS)

Two of the common characteristics of questions in English are also common in Spanish: They often begin with a word to indicate what follows is a question, and they usually use a word order that is different than that usually used in direct statements.

The first thing you may notice about written Spanish questions is a punctuation difference; they always begin with an inverted question mark (¿). The question-indicating words, known as interrogatives, all have their equivalents in English:

- *qué*: what
- *por qué*: why
- *cuándo*: when
- *dónde*: where
- *cómo*: how
- *cuál, cuáles*: which
- *quién, quiénes*: who
- *cuánto, cuánta*: how much
- *cuántos, cuántas*: how many

Although the English equivalents are the most common ones used to translate these words, other translations are sometimes possible. Several of these interrogatives can be preceded by prepositions: *a quién* (to whom), *de quién* (of whom), *de dónde* (from where), *de qué* (of what), etc. Note that all these words have accents; generally, when the same words are used in statements, they do not have accents. There is no difference in pronunciation. Generally, a verb follows the interrogative.

>¿Qué es eso? (What is that?)
>¿Por qué fue a la ciudad? (Why did he go to the city?)
>¿Qué es la capital del Perú? (What is the capital of Peru?)
>¿Dónde está mi coche? (Where is my car?)

When the verb needs a subject other than the interrogative, it follows the verb:

- ¿Por qué fue él a la ciudad? (Why did he go to the city?)

- *¿Cuántos dólares tiene el muchacho?* (How many dollars does the boy have?)

As in English, questions can be formed in Spanish without the interrogatives, although Spanish is more flexible in its word order. In Spanish, the general form is for the noun to follow the verb. The noun can either appear immediately after the verb or appear later in the sentence. In the following examples, either Spanish question is a grammatically valid way of expressing the English:

- *¿Va Pedro al mercado? ¿Va al mercado Pedro?* (Is Pedro going to the market?)
- *¿Tiene que ir Roberto al banco? ¿Tiene que ir al banco Roberto?* (Does Roberto have to go to the bank?)
- *¿Sale María mañana? ¿Sale mañana María?* (Is María leaving tomorrow?)

As you can see, Spanish doesn't require auxiliary verbs the way that English does to form questions.

Also, as in English, a statement can be made into a question simply by a change in intonation (the voice tone) or, in writing, by adding question marks, although it isn't particularly common. *Él es doctor.* He's a doctor. *¿Él es doctor?* He's a doctor? Finally, note that when only part of a sentence is a question, in Spanish the question marks are placed around only the portion that's a question:

- *Estoy feliz, ¿y tú?* (I'm happy, are you?)
- *Si salgo, ¿salen ellos también?* (If I leave, are they leaving too?)

PRÁCTICA

Insert the correct interrogative (question word).
List: *Qué, Quién, Cómo, Cuándo, Por qué, Cuánto/a/os/as, Cuál, Dónde*

1. ¿_____hora es?
2. ¿_____te llamas?
3. ¿De _____eres?
4. ¿_____es tu color favorito?
5. ¿_____vives?
6. ¿_____vas a la escuela? ¿En coche o en autobús?
7. ¿_____empieza la clase de español? ¿Por la mañana o después del mediodía?
8. ¿_____tiempo hace?
9. ¿_____personas hay en tu familia?
10. ¿_____es tu familia? ¿Es grande o pequeña?
11. ¿_____está la biblioteca? ¿Lejos o cerca?
12. ¿_____quieres comer? ¿Pizza o hamburguesa?
13. ¿_____años tienes?
14. ¿A_____vas?
15. ¿_____es tu número de teléfono?
16. ¿_____es tu cumpleaños?
17. ¿_____eres? ¿Eres amable o antipático?
18. ¿_____es tu mejor amigo? ¿Es Juan o Frederico?
19. ¿_____es la fecha de hoy?
20. ¿_____ pesos cuesta el sándwich?

CAPÍTULO OCHO:
SUBJECT PRONOUNS

Subject Pronouns are used to talk to and about people. Here are the subject pronouns in Spanish:

	SINGULAR		PLURAL	
1st Person	**Yo**	I	**nosotros/as**	we
2nd Person	**Tú**	You (familiar)	**vosotros/as**	you all familiar
3rd Person	**Él** **Ella** **Ud.(usted)**	He She You (formal)	**ellos** **ellas** **Uds.(ustedes)**	they (masculine) they (feminine) you all formal

Notice that *nosotros/nosotras* is across from *yo; vosotros/vosotras* is across from *tú; él* is across from *ellos; ella* is across from *ellas;* and *usted* is across from *ustedes*. It is important to maintain this form when you write the pronouns in a conjugation chart. Verbs are always conjugated in the above order; it's imperative that you know this chart in order to conjugate any verb that you come across.

The pronouns listed above are arranged in a chart form that is used for grammatical explanations. Grammatical terms such as "first person singular" or "third person plural" are often used to identify pronouns listed in a specific order. Each different pronoun case is listed in the same order as the subject pronouns listed above. Any new pronoun case presented in this book will be in the same order as the subject case.

Yo (I) refers to the person speaking, tú refers to the person spoken to, and él or ella (he, she) to the person spoken about. (The subject pronoun "it" in English is never expressed in Spanish, but is included in the 3rd person singular form of the verb.)

Examples:

Yo soy Miguel	I am Miguel.
Ella no es la professor.	She is not the professor.
¿Quién eres tú?	Who are you?
¿Es usted el Sr. Ramos?	Are you Sr. Ramos?

Yo is not capitalized unless it is at the beginning of the sentence.

Tú and usted both mean you. Tú is the familiar form of address usually children family and friends. Usted is used to show respect or indicate a more formal relationship with the person addressed. Customarily usted is used to to address teachers, elders and adults you don't know well.

Vosotros is when the group of "you all" being addressed is familiar. **Uds.** is when the group of "you all" is formal.

Vosotros, nosotros and ellos are masculine, or when the group is a mixture of males and females.

PRÁCTICA

Which of the following subject pronouns would you use to talk about the following people?

Modelo: Carlos y yo; Nosotros

1. Carlotta y Maria
2. Mi amiga y yo
3. Manuel y Andrés
4. Tú y tú
5. Los chicos y las chicas
6. El profesor
7. Usted y yo
8. Tú y Juan
9. Tú y yo
10. El señor y las señoras

Capítulo Nueve:
Regular Verbs

All Spanish verbs are either "regular" or "irregular." In this lesson we will look at three completely regular verbs:

hablar (to speak)
comer (to eat)
vivir (to live)

Notice the last two letters of each verb.

habl**ar** (to speak)
com**er** (to eat)
viv**ir** (to live)

There are three categories of verbs:

-ar verbs (like hablar)
-er verbs (like comer)
-ir verbs (like vivir)

All three categories are infinitives. Infinitives are the base form of the verb, equivalent in English to: to speak, to eat, to live, etc. ***In Spanish, all infinitives end in -ar, -er, or -ir.***

-ar verb
hablar (to speak)

-er verb
comer (to eat)

-ir verb
vivir (to live)

When you conjugate a verb, you change its form depending on the subject so that it is grammatically correct. This is done in English as well as Spanish.

to speak

I speak
you speak
he speaks
she speaks
we speak
you-all speak
they speak

Now, note the Spanish forms:

hablar - to speak

yo hablo	I speak
tú hablas	you (familiar) speak
él/ella, usted habla	He/she/you/it speaks
nosotros/as hablamos	we speak
vosotros/as habláis	you all (familiar) speak
ellos/ellas/ustedes hablan	they/you all speak

comer - to eat

yo como	I eat
tú comes	you (familiar) eat
él/ella, usted come	He/she/you/it eats
nosotros/as comemos	we eat
vosotros/as coméis	you all (familiar) eat
ellos/ellas/ustedes comen	they/you-all eat

vivir - to live

yo vivo	I live
tú vives	you (familiar) live
él/ella, usted vive	He/she/you/it lives
nosotros/as vivimos	we live
vosotros/as vivís	you all (familiar) live
ellos/ellas/ustedes viven	they/you-all live

CAPÍTULO NUEVE   47

Note the pattern in the yo form.

yo habl_o_
yo com_o_
yo viv_o_

If the subject is I (yo), conjugate by dropping the ending and add -o.

yo hablo **(hablar - ar + o = hablo)**
yo como **(comer - er + o = como)**
yo vivo **(vivir - ir + o = vivo)**

Note the pattern in the usted form.

usted habl_a_
usted com_e_
usted viv_e_

If the subject is you formal (usted) drop the ending and add either -a or -e. If the verb is an -ar verb, add -a. If it is an -er or -ir verb, add -e.

usted habla **(hablar - ar + a = habla)**
usted come **(comer - er + e = come)**
usted vive **(vivir - ir + e = vive)**

Note the pattern in the nosotros/as form.

nosotros/as habl_amos_
nosotros/as com_emos_
nosotros/as viv_imos_

If the subject is we (nosotros/as), conjugate by dropping the ending and add -amos, -emos, or -imos.

Notice that the ending of the infinitive determines which is used: -ar verbs add -amos, -er verbs add -emos, -ir verbs add -imos.

nosotros/as hablamos
(hablar - ar + amos = hablamos)

nosotros/as comemos
(comer - er + emos = comemos)

nosotros/as vivimos
(vivir - ir + imos = vivimos)

Note the pattern in the ustedes form.

ustedes habl_an_, ustedes com_en_, ustedes viv_en_

If the subject is you-all (ustedes), conjugate by dropping the ending and add -an or -en. If the verb is an -ar verb, add -an. If it is an -er or an -ir verb, add -en.

ustedes hablan
(hablar - ar + an = hablan)

ustedes comen
(comer - er + en = comen)

ustedes viven
(vivir - ir + en = viven)

Present tense (indicative) in Spanish means three things.

1. **Yo hablo inglés.**
   I speak English.
   I do speak English.
   I am speaking English.

2. **Yo como pan.**
   I eat bread.
   I do eat bread.
   I am eating bread.

3. **Yo vivo en Buenos Aires.**
   I live in Buenos Aires.
   I do live in Buenos Aires.
   I am living in Buenos Aires.

In summary, in order to conjugate a regular verb, you simply drop the ending and add the following letters to the stem/root of the verb:

AR Verbs

Yo- O	Nosotros(as)-AMOS
Tú-AS	Vosotros(as)-ÁIS
Él-A Ella -A Usted-A (it)	Ellos-AN Ellas-AN Ustedes-AN

ER Verbs

Yo- O	Nosotros(as)-EMOS
Tú-ES	Vosotros(as)-ÉIS
Él-E Ella -E Ud. –E (it)	Ellos-EN Ellas-EN Ustedes-EN

IR Verbs

Yo- O	Nosotros(as)-IMOS
Tú-ES	Vosotros(as)-ÍS
Él-E Ella -E Ud. –E (it)	Ellos-EN Ellas-EN Ustedes-EN

Conjugations of Common Regular Spanish Verbs

Verb	Yo	Tú	Él, Ella Usted	Nosotros	Vosotros	Ellos, Ellas, Ustedes
Bailar	Bailo	Bailas	Baila	Bailamos	Bailáis	Bailan
Eschuchar	Escucho	Escuchas	Escucha	Escuchamos	Escucháis	Escuchan
Comer	Como	Comes	Come	Comemos	Coméis	Comen
Leer	Leo	Lees	Lee	Leemos	leéis	Leen
Escribir	Escribo	Escribes	Escribe	Escribimos	Escribís	Escriben
Mirar	Miro	Miras	Mira	Miramos	Miráis	Miran
Subir	Subo	Subes	Sube	Subimos	Subís	Suben
Correr	Corro	Corres	Corre	Corremos	Corréis	Corren
Limpiar	Limpio	Limpias	Limpia	Limpiamos	Limpáis	Limpian
Tomar	Tomo	Tomas	Toma	Tomamos	Tomáis	Toman
Hablar	Hablo	Hablas	Habla	Hablamos	Habláis	Hablan

Common Regular -ar Verbs

alquilar – to rent
entrar (en) – to enter (into)
necesitar – to need
amar – to love
enviar – to send
andar – to walk
escuchar – to listen to

pagar – to pay for
ayudar – to help
esperar – to hope, to wait for
practicar – to practice
bailar – to dance
estudiar – to study
preguntar – to ask
buscar – to look for
preparar – to prepare
caminar – to walk
ganar – to win, earn
regresar – to return
cantar – to sing
saludar – to greet
cocinar – to cook
hablar – to speak, to talk
tocar – to touch, to play an instrument
comprar – to buy
lavar – to wash
tomar – to take, to drink
contestar – to answer
llegar – to arrive
trabajar – to work
dejar – to allow, to leave
llevar – to wear, to carry
viajar – to travel
desear – to desire
visitar – to visit
enseñar – to teach
mirar – to watch, to look at

Common Regular -er Verbs

aprender – to learn
creer – to believe
poseer – to possess, to own
beber – to drink
deber – to have to, to owe
prometer – to promise
comer – to eat
esconder – to hide
romper – to break
comprender – to understand
leer – to read
temer – to fear
correr – to run
meter en – to put into
vender – to sell

CAPÍTULO NUEVE   51

Common Regular -ir Verbs

abrir – to open
descubrir – to discover
permitir – to permit
admitir – to admit
discutir – to discuss
recibir – to receive
asistir a – to attend
escribir – to write
subir – to climb, to go up
cubrir – to cover
existir – to exist
sufrir – to suffer
decidir – to decide
omitir – to omit
unir – to unite
describir – to describe
partir – to divide
vivir – to live

PRÁCTICA
Combine the two columns to make a sentence.

1) Mi amiga Claudia   estudiar para los exámenes

2) Hector y Manuel   escribir papeles

3) Tú   vivir en Los Estados Unidos

4) Mi amiga y yo   leer libros

5) Yo   escuchar la música

6) Luisa   comer mucho

7) Usted   beber mucha agua

8) Ellos   trabajar en Walmart

9) Ustedes   tomar café

10) Juan y Carlos   tocar la flauta

11) Mi familia   asistir a la fiesta

12) Juan Carlos y yo   estudiar en la biblioteca

Fill in the blanks with the correct form of the verbs

1. Tú (vivir) _____ con tus padres.
a. vivas   b. vive   c. vives   d. vivimos

2. Yo (hablar) _____ español.
a. hablo   b. hable   c. hablamos   d. hablas

3. Ellos (comer) _____ muy temprano.
a. come   b. comen   c. como   d. comes

4. Nosotros (bailar) _____ el tango.
a. bailamos   b. bailas   c. bailan   d. bailo

5. Usted (cantar) _____ muy bien.
a. cantas   b. canta   c. cante   d. cantamos

6. ¿Tú (correr) _____ por las mañanas?
a. corres   b. corre   c. corras   d. corremos

7. Ella (escribir) _____ cartas muy largas.
a. escribo   b. escriba   c. escribe   d. escribimos

8. Él (asistir) _____ a la escuela todos los día
a. asisto   b. asiste   c. asistes   d. asista

9. Ustedes no (ver) _____ a la televisión.
a. veen   b. ven   c. ves   d. vemos

10. Nosotros (leer) _____ el periódico.
a. leemos   b. lean   c. lees   d. lemos

CAPÍTULO DIEZ:
SER VS. ESTAR

Ser and estar both mean "to be" and are irregular verbs. They are not interchangeable, so you must learn when you use which one.

We use Ser for the following things:
- Time
- Date
- Characteristics

Physical (don't change from day to day)
Personality (again, not easily changed)

- Profession
- Origin

These are the forms of SER in the present tense.

yo **soy**	nosotros **somos**
tú **eres**	vosotros **sois**
él, ella, usted **es**	ellos, ellas, ustedes **son**

Ejemplos:
Time	Son las dos y media.
Date	Es el diez de enero.
Characteristics	Somos guapos.
	Eres inteligente.
Profession	Soy profesor.
Origin	Ella es de Chile.

We use Estar for the following things:
- Present Location
- Feelings/Emotions
- Physical (sick, well, tired, etc.)
- Temporary Conditions

Can change from moment to moment

These are the forms of ESTAR in the present tense.

yo **estoy**	nosotros **estamos**
tú **estás**	vosotros **estáis**
él, ella, usted **está**	ellos, ellas, ustedes **está**

Ejemplos:
Present Location
-People
-Things

Estoy en clase.
La escuela está en Watertown.

Feelings
--Physical
--Emotional

Estamos bien.
Estás aburrido.

Temporary Conditions

El agua está caliente.

PRÁCTICA

Decide whether to use Ser or Estar, then conjugate accordingly.

1) Yo _____ de los Estados Unidos. (I am from the USA.)

2) Ella _____ en el baño. (She is in the bathroom.)

3) Nosotros no _____ muy inteligentes. (We aren't very smart.)

4) Tú _____ médico. (You are a doctor.)

5) La familia no _____ en casa. (The familiy is not home.)

6) Mis padres _____ dominicanos. (My parents are Dominican.)

7) Él _____ enfermo. (He is sick.)

8) ¿ _____ Uds. preparando el postre? (Are you preparing dessert?)

9) Mi hermana y yo _____ actores. (My sister and I are actors.)

10) Alba no _____ tonta. (Alba isn't foolish.)

11) Nosotros _____ cansados. (We are tired.)

12) Mi vecino _____ muy alto. (My neighbor is very tall.)

13) ¿ _____ tú bien? (Are you well?)

14) Yo _____ un estudiante. (I am a student.)

CÁPITULO DIEZ   55

15) Ellos no _____ escuchando la música. (They aren't listening to music.)

16) ¿_____ Maria y José en la playa? (Are Mary and Joe at the beach?)

17) El camarero _____ en la cocina. (The waiter is in the kitchen.)

18) Nosotras no _____ de Cuba. (We are not from Cuba.)

I. Would you use **ser** or **estar** to talk about the following things? Write **ser** or **estar** next to the each one and then write a sentence in Spanish for each of the nine categories based on your life.

A.
1. possession
2. someone's current condition
3. nationality or origin
4. location
5. inherent traits
6. event location
7. identifying someone or something
8. actions in progress
9. time

B.
1. _____

2. _____

3. _____

4. _____

5. _____

6. _____

7. _____

8. _____

9. _____

II. Read the sentences and decide if you would use **ser** or **estar** for each. Do not translate the sentences, just write **ser** or **estar** and explain your reasons.

La boda (The wedding)
1. Who is that gorgeous guy?
2. The bride is beautiful.
3. Yes, and the groom looks handsome in this tux.
4. Where is the father of the bride?
5. He's in the bar across the street.
6. He's furious because weddings are so expensive.
7. When is the ceremony?
8. It's at 4:00.
9. It's hard to see the bride from here.
10. Which one is the bride's mother?
11. She is dressed in a red suit.
12. She's very emotional.
13. What day is today?
14. It's Saint Valentine's Day, how romantic for the wedding!
15. Where is the groom from?
16. He's from Seattle.
17. They are saying their vows at this very moment.
18. I'm so happy that I could cry.
19. Where is the reception?
20. In the restaurant that is right next to the bar across the street.

CAPÍTULO ONCE: STEM-CHANGING/BOOT VERBS & VERBS WITH IRREGULAR "YO FORMS

Ah, those famous -- or is it '*infamous*'? – stem-changing or **boot-verbs** (sometimes called "shoe verbs" by folks who aren't from farming or ranching country). This category of verbs is made up of a small number of -AR, -ER, -IR verbs. The only difference between the verbs that fit into the category of "boot verbs," and all the other verbs you've been working with up until now, is this: when you conjugate these boot-verbs, the conjugations that fits inside my mythical "boot" -- which I'll show you here in a second -- has its *stem* vowel changed from a single vowel to a double vowel, i.e., the "u" in the verb jugar (to play a game) has to be changed to "**ue**" for the following conjugations:

juego	jugamos
juegas	jugaís
juega	Juegan

The same rule holds true for the e that needs to stem-change to ie . . . the o that needs to stem-change to ue . . . and the e that has to stem-change to i in other verbs classified as boot-verbs.

What's the "stem of a verb," you ask? Well, here is how I would explain it.
. . . To understand what the "stem" is, we need to need to examine, and to be able to identify, all the possible parts of a verb. Spanish boot-verbs, like non-boot verbs, can be made up of up to three (3) different elements. These elements (or "parts," if you prefer) are, in order, from the beginning to the end of the verb:

1. the **prefix**.
2. the **stem (or the *root*, as it's sometimes called)**.
3. the **ending**.

As an example, let's use the boot-verb preferir (i, i). * If we were to break it down according to the above-mentioned, we find that the prefix is pre-, the stem is fer, and the ending is -ir. In a boot-verb, it is the *stem* that undergoes the spelling change when the verb is conjugated into the present tense.

You will remember that all Spanish verbs end in either "-AR," "-ER," "-IR." So, in other words, the part of the verb that comes right before the verb end is called the "stem" of the verb, and the 'stem' of the verb is that part of the verb that isn't

1. the verb identifier, that is the "-AR," the "-ER," the "-IR".

2. the prefix part, that is, *dis, pre, re, ob, con, com*, among others.

It seem a bit weird, but when I was first learning these "boot verbs," I came up my own rule of thumb for figuring out which vowel was supposed to be changed . . . maybe it will be helpful to you (or . . . maybe it won't!) I decided that the way to figure out and remember which vowel was the "stem-changer" in these verbs was to first find the "-AR," the "-ER," the" -IR" ending -- not too difficult, even for a bonehead like me!! -- then move my eyes back toward the front of the verb, and when I found the very next vowel, that is, the vowel closest to the verb end, that vowel was the one that got changed within the "boot." Here's a list of what I think are some of the most common boot-verbs we might use on a daily basis. As you will see, I've tried to divide them into their stem-changing groups: **u --> ue**, **o --> ue**; **e --> ie**; and **e --> i**.

e --> ie

preferir (ie, i) -- to prefer

querer (ie) — to want; to love

divertir (ie, i) — to entertain somone

sugerir (ie) -- to suggest

obtener (i, i) * -- to obtain, to get

tener (i, i)* -- to have; to be (years old)

divertirse (ie, i) — to enjoy oneself

e --> i

servir (i, i) -- to serve

vestirse (i, i) -- to get dressed

vestir (i, i) — to dress someone

reírse (i, i) — to laugh

despedirse de (i, i) — to say "good-bye" to

Pedir(e-i) to ask for

conseguir + infinitive (i, i) — to succed in doing something

sonreírse (i, i) — to smile

o --> ue

dormir (ue, u) -- to sleep

poder (ue) -- to be able to do something)

morirse (ue, u) -- to die

dormir (ue, u) -- to fall asleep

almorzar (ue, u) -- to eat lunch

u --> ue

jugar (ue) -- to play a game

Now, we've been calling these verbs both "stem-changers" and "boot-verbs", right? Let's do some drawings and see how it is that the word "boot" and the word "boot" end up in the same sentence. We'll start with that most common of verbs: *querer*-- to want/wish/love. Our first order of business will be to mentally construct our "boot." You know, when you're first starting to work with these bad boys, drawing out a boot on a piece of paper is really helpful tool. We'll conjugate it and you'll see how the "boot" idea came into being to describe these verbs:

ER verbs like *comer, beber, aprender* and the like:

```
       -o  -emos
       -es -éis
       -e  -en
```

The same endings we use for present tense, regular -AR verbs:

```
       -o -amos
       -as -áis
       -a -an
```

present tense, regular -IR verbs:

```
       -o -imos
       -es -ís
       -e -en
```

Here are a few more of the verbs you'll likely use in your travels to México . . . and beyond:

"E" changes to "IE"

- *entender* -- to understand
- *cerrar* -- to close (*something*)
- *pensar* -- to think
- *comenzar* -- to commence or to begin
- *empezar* -- to start or to begin
- *perder* -- to lose (a game, your keys, etc.)

"O" goes to "UE"

- *volver* -- to return
- *costar* -- to cost
- *llover* -- to rain

Here's the main "U goes to UE" verb

"U" goes to "UE"

***jugar* -- to play (board games, athletics)**

PRÁCTICA

Llena el espacio en blanco con la forma correcta del verbo.

1. Tú _____ a clase a tiempo todos los días? (VENIR (e-i).

2,3. Ellos _____ al golf, pero nosotros _____ al tenís (JUGAR, JUGAR).

4. Mis padres _____ su viaje a Salem, Oregon esta noche (COMENZAR e-ie).

5. Teresa _____ que estudiar para el examen (TENER e-ie).

6. Brad _____ a clase cada día (VENIR e-ie).

7. Chandra y Shelly no _____ mucho tiempo para festejar (TENER e-ie).

8. Dave _____ más comer pizza que jamón (PREFERIR e-ie).

9. Yo _____ a estudiar muy temprano: a las 6:00 a.m. (COMENZAR e-ie).

10. Megan _____ las llaves ¿no es así? (PERDER e-ie).

11. Alex y yo _____ en la clase de Español. (DORMIR o-ue)

12. Alejandro _____ a casa a las once. (VOLVER o-ue)

13. Kevin y yo _____ ganar el campeonato de ajedrez (QUERER).

14. Mi novia_____la puerta de mi coche con demasiada fuerza (CERRAR).

15. Nosotros no_____la lección (ENTENDER).

The following verbs have irregular forms for the first person singular of the present tense:

caber (to fit)
    yo quepo
caer (to fall)
    yo caigo
conducir (to drive)
    yo conduzco
conocer (to know, to be acquainted with)
    yo conozco
escoger (to choose)
    yo escojo
dirigir (to direct)
    yo dirijo
hacer (to do, to make)
    yo hago
poner (to put, to place)
    yo pongo
saber (to know something - a fact)
    yo sé

salir (to leave)
    yo salgo

seguir (to follow)
    yo sigo
traer (to bring)
    yo traigo
ttener
    yo tengo
valer (to be worth)
    yo valgo
venir
    yo vengo
ver (to see)
    yo veo

In addition to memorizing the above listed verbs, you should familiarize yourself with the following three rules:

1. For verbs that end in -cer and -cir, change the **c** to **zc** for the yo form:

conocer (to know)
yo conozco

conducir (to drive)
yo conduzco

crecer (to grow)
yo crezco

traducir (to translate)
yo traduzco

establecer (to establish)
yo establezco

producir (to produce)
yo produzco

2. For verbs that end in -ger and -gir, change the **g** to **j** for the yo form:

escoger (to choose)
yo escojo

dirigir (to direct)
yo dirijo

emerger (to emerge)
yo emerjo

fingir (to pretend)
yo finjo

3. For verbs that end in -guir, change the **gu** to **g** for the yo form:

seguir (to follow)
yo sigo

conseguir (to get)
yo consigo

distinguir (to distinguish)
yo distingo

CAPÍTULO DOCE:
DIRECT AND INDIRECT OBJECTS AND THE PERSONAL "A"

Direct-object pronouns are those pronouns that represent the nouns directly acted upon by the verb. Indirect-object pronouns stand for the noun that is the recipient of the verb's action. In both English and Spanish, a verbs may have no object (e.g., "I live," *vivo*), a direct object only (e.g., "I killed the fly," *maté la mosca*), or both direct and indirect objects (e.g., "I gave her the ring," *le di el anillo*). The construction of an indirect object without a direct object isn't used in English, but it can be done in Spanish (e.g., *le es difícil*, "it is difficult for him.")

In the second example, the direct object of the verb is "the ring" (*el anillo*), because it is what was given. The indirect object is "her," (or *le*) because the person is the recipient of the giving.

Another way of looking at indirect objects in Spanish is that they could be replaced by "*a* + prepositional pronoun" or sometimes "*para* + prepositional pronoun." In the example sentence, we could say *di el anillo a ella* and mean the same thing (just as we could say in English, "I gave the ring to her") In Spanish, unlike English, a noun can't be an indirect object; it must be used as prepositional pronoun. For example, we could say "I gave Sally the ring" in English, but in Spanish the preposition *a* is needed, *di el anillo a Sally*.) Similarly, note also that in Spanish that the indirect object pronoun must refer to a person or animal.

In English, we use the same pronouns for both direct and indirect objects. In Spanish, both types of object pronouns are the same except in the third person. The third-person singular direct object pronouns are *lo* (masculine) and *la* (feminine), while in the plural, they are *los* and *las*. But the indirect object pronouns are *le* and *les* in singular and plural, respectively. No distinction is made according to gender.

The other object pronouns in Spanish are *me* (first-person singular), *te* (second-person familiar singular), *nos* (first-person plural) and *os* (second-person familiar plural). The following chart forms are the object pronouns in Spanish.

Direct Object pronouns

me	*me*	*Ella me ve* (she sees me).
you (familiar)	*te*	*Ella te ve.*
him, her, it, you (formal)	*lo* (masculine) *la* (feminine)	*Ella lo/la ve.*
us	*nos*	*Ella nos ve.*
you (familiar plural)	*os*	*Ella os ve.*
them, you (plural formal)	*los* (masculine) *las* (feminine)	*Ella los/las ve.*

Indirect objects are the people or things in a sentence to whom/what or the action of the verb occurs.

I'm talking to José. - Hablo a José.
To whom am I talking? José.

He gives books to the students - Da unos libros a los estudiantes.
To whom does he give books? - The students.

Indirect object pronouns are the words that replace the indirect object, which is usually a person.

The Spanish indirect object pronouns are as follows:

SUBJECT	INDIRECT OBJ.
YO	ME
TÚ	TE
USTED	LE
ÉL	LE
ELLA	LE
NOSOTROS	NOS
USTEDES	LES
ELLOS	LES
ELLAS	LES

Like direct object pronouns, Spanish indirect object pronouns are placed in front of the verb.

I'm talking to him. - Le hablo.
He writes to them - Les escribe.
I'm giving the bread to you. - Te doy el pan.
She answered me - Ella me contestó.

For infinitives, present participles and affirmative commands, pronouns can get attached to the end.

Le voy a decir or Voy a decirle - I'm going to tell him.
Les quiero traer el regalo or Quiero traerles el regalo - I want to bring the gift to them.

Note: When deciding between direct and indirect objects, the general rule is that if the person or thing is preceded by a preposition (with the exception of the personal a) that person/thing is an indirect object. If it is not preceded by a preposition, it is a direct object.

Se: To avoid alliteration, when le or les as an indirect-object pronoun precedes the direct-object pronoun lo, los, la or las, se is used instead of le or les. Quiero dárselo, I want to give it to him (or her or you). Se lo daré, I will give it to him (or her or you).

Placement of object pronouns after verbs:

Object pronouns are placed after infinitives (the unconjugated form of the verb that ends in -ar, -er or -ir), gerunds (the form of the verb that ends in -ando or -endo, generally equivalent to the "-ing" ending in English), and the affirmative imperative. *Quiero abrirla*, I want to open it. *No estoy abriéndola*, I am not opening it. *Ábrela*, open it. Note that where the pronunciation requires it, an orthographic accent needs to be added to the verb.

Placement of object pronouns before verbs:

Object pronouns are placed before verb forms except those listed above, in other words, after nearly all the conjugated forms. *Quiero que la abras*, I want you to open is. *No la abro*, I am not opening it. *No la abras*, don't open it.

Order of object pronouns:

When both direct-object and indirect-object pronouns are objects of the same verb, the indirect object comes before the direct object. *Me lo dará*, he will give it to me. *Quiero dártelo*, I want to give it to you.

PRÁCTICA

Re-write the sentences with the correct direct object.

Modelo: El chico manda la carta a su abuela.   <u>El chico la manda a su abuela.</u>

1. Compramos los guantes (gloves) en Walmart.

2. Yo leo un libro.
3. Juanita usa la crema protectora. (sunscreen)
4. Escuchamos la radio.
5. Llevo los anteojos. (sunglasses)
6. Compré los zapatos. (shoes)
7. El estudiante necesita su calculadora.
8. No veo las muchachas.
9. Busco las raquetas.

Fill in the blanks with the correct direct objects
10. Yo no vi el programa. >> Yo no _____ vi.

11. Isabel nos trajo la sal y la pimienta. >> Isabel nos _____ trajo.

12. Perdón, yo no pedí papas con el bistec. >> Perdón, yo no _____ pedí con el bistec.

13. ¿Quién te recomendó este restaurante? >> ¿Quién te _____ recomendó?

14. Dejé mi cartera en el coche. >> _____ dejé en el coche.

15. ¿Viste a nosotros en el cine ayer? >> ¿_____ viste en el cine ayer?

16. No, no vi a Uds. ayer. >> No, no _____ vi ayer.

17. Quise llamar a ti pero no estuviste. >> Quise llamar___ pero no estuviste.

18. ¿A qué hora buscaste a mi? >> ¿A qué hora _____ buscaste?

19. Papá, _____ compré (a ti) una corbata para tu cumpleaños.

20. Gracias, hijo. _____ doy (a ti) un abrazo.

21. _____ escribí unas postales a mis padres cuando estaba de vacaciones.

22. ¿_____ puedes prestar *(lend) (a mí)* 1.000 pesos?

23. Sí, _____ los puedo prestar *(a ti)* hoy, pero tú _____ tienes que devolver *(return) (a mí)* la semana que viene.

24. _____ envié correo electrónico *a mis amigos* en México. _____ escribo frecuentemente.

25. Por favor, señorita, ¿_____ trae la cuenta *a nosotros*?

A. Determine the direct object (DO) and the indirect object (IO). Write only the noun, not the article.

He gave her the ring.

1. DO=_____

2. IO=_____

He sang them a song.

3. DO=_____

4. IO=_____

Give the dog a bone.

5. DO=_____

6. IO=_____

Substitute the correct pronoun.

7. Juan compra flores para ella.
Juan_____compra flores.

8. El mesero da el menú a ellos.
El mesero_____da el menú.

9. Ellos dan una propina a mí.
Ellos_____dan una propina.

10. Compro el libro para ti.
_____ compro el libro.

The Personal "A"

The direct object is the noun or pronoun that receives the action of the verb. In the following sentences, the direct objects are underlined.

Mike hit the <u>ball</u>.
George calls <u>Mary</u>.
He calls <u>her</u>.

In Spanish, when the direct object is a person, it is preceded by the preposition "a." This word has no English translation.

Jorge llama <u>a</u> María.
Jorge calls María.

From the perspective of the English speaker, the personal "a" appears to be an extra word. From the perspective of the Spanish speaker, the personal "a" is required and to not use it is a serious error.

Jorge llama <u>a</u> María.

The personal "a" may also be used if the direct object is a domesticated animal, especially a pet, provided that the speaker attaches some sort of personal feelings towards the animal.

La mujer acaricia <u>a</u> su perro. (acariciar)
The woman pets her dog.

El perro persigue <u>a</u> la gata. (perseguir)
The dog chases the cat.

The personal "a" is not used when the direct object is not a person or is an animal for which no personal feelings are felt.

Bebo la leche. (beber)
I drink the milk. -- milk is neither a person nor an animal

Miro la jirafa. (mirar)
I look at the giraffe. -- no personal feelings are felt towards the giraffe

The personal "a" is not used after the verb tener, or the verb form hay. This is true even if the direct object is a person.

Tengo dos hermanos. (tener)
I have two brothers.

Hay cinco chicas.
There are five girls.

CAPÍTULO DOCE

If the direct object is an indefinite person, the personal "a" is not used. The result is that the person becomes "depersonalized."

Necesito médico.
I need (any) doctor. (or)
I need medical assistance.

Necesito jardinero.
I need (any) gardener. (or)
I need someone to tend my garden.

Because this Spanish grammatical structure has no equivalent in English, it is normal to expect that the student will forget to use it until a pattern of use has been established. Remember, to not use the personal "a" is a serious error, and the student should try to remember to use it when appropriate.

CAPÍTULO TRECE:
"I LIKE IT; I LOVE IT"

GUSTAR AND VERBS LIKE GUSTAR

This is a good time to discuss the verb "gustar" because using it requires use of the IO pronouns.

Me gusta el cuarto.
I like the room.

Nos gustan los libros.
We like the books.

In English, the following sentences are correct:

I like the room.
We like the books.

Examine the same sentences more closely.

I like the room.

I = subject of sentence
like = verb
the room = direct object

We like the books.

We = subject of sentence
like = verb
the books = direct object

In English, it is correct to construct a sentence that has the subject "liking" a direct object. **In Spanish, this never occurs.** In Spanish, a different construction is used.

English: I like the room.
Spanish: The room is pleasing to me.

English: We like the books.
Spanish: The books are pleasing to us.

The first thing you need to notice is that both versions really mean the same thing. They are merely different expressions of the same idea.

Idea: My feelings with regard to the book are positive.

English Way: I like the book.
Spanish Way: The book is pleasing to me.

The second thing to notice is that in English, the subject of the sentence is the person (I, we) while in Spanish the subject of the sentence is the object (room, books).

The room is pleasing to me.
Subject: The room

I like the room.
Subject: I

Finally notice that while the English sentence has a direct object, the Spanish sentence has an indirect object.

The room is pleasing to me.
me = Indirect Object

I like the room.
room = Direct Object

Let's study the following example:

Me gustan los libros.

Literal Translation: To me are pleasing the books.
Actual Translation: I like the books.

Notice that gustar is conjugated as "gustan" **not** "gusto." A common mistake is to say "Me gusto los libros." This is incorrect because the subject of the sentence is "los libros" even though it comes at the end. Remember, the verb is conjugated to agree with the subject of the sentence.

Me **gustan** los libros. (I like the books.)

Notice that the conjugation of gustar changes to "gusta" when the subject of the sentence is singular.

Me **gusta** el libro. (I like the book.)

Since the subject of the sentence must be either singular (book) or plural (books), the only forms of gustar you will use are "gusta" and "gustan." This is true regardless of what IO pronoun appears in the sentence.

Me gusta el libro.
I like the book.

Te gusta el libro.
You like the book.

Nos gusta el libro.
We like the book.

Me gustan los libros.
I like the books.

Te gustan los libros.
You like the books.

Remember, gustar becomes either gusta or gustan, depending upon whether the subject of the sentence is singular or plural. It has nothing to do with which IO pronoun is used.

Subject is singular - use gusta

Me gusta el libro.
Te gusta el libro.

Subject is plural - use gustan

Me gustan los libros.
Te gustan los libros.

Remember, the IO pronoun is **not** the subject of the sentence!

Nos gustamos ... **incorrect!**
Te gustas ... **incorrect!**

Here are some examples of the correct use of gustar. Notice that the only forms of gustar that appear are gusta and gustan, even though each of the IO pronouns is used.

Singular Subject	**Plural Subject**
Me gusta la casa.	Me gustan las casas.
Te gusta el cuarto.	Te gustan los cuartos.
Le gusta la silla.	Le gustan las sillas.
Nos gusta el hotel.	Nos gustan los hoteles.
Os gusta la comida.	Os gustan las comidas.
Les gusta el reloj.	Les gustan los relojes.

Look more closely at one example:

Le gusta la silla.

    It is impossible to tell whether this means:

    1. He likes the chair.

    2. She likes the chair.

3. You (usted) like the chair.

For purposes of clarification, the sentence will often begin with a prepositional phrase that clarifies just who the IO pronoun refers to.

A él le gusta la silla.
He likes the chair.

A Juan le gusta la silla.
John likes the chair.

A ella le gusta la silla.
She likes the chair.

A María le gusta la silla.
Mary likes the chair.

A usted le gusta la silla.
You (formal) like the chair.

As you can see, by adding a prepositional phrase, we remove the ambiguity of the "le" form. You can also use a prepositional phrase to add emphasis, even if there is no ambiguity.

1. A Juan le gusta el café.
John likes coffee.

2. A mí me gusta el té.
I like tea.

In the first example, "a Juan" clarifies the ambiguous pronoun "le." In the second example, there is no ambiguity. "Me gusta el té" can only mean "I like tea." In this case, "a mí" adds emphasis, drawing attention to the fact that tea is what I like (as contrasted with what Juan likes).

Another way to look at it:

John likes coffee. Me, I like tea.
A Juan le gusta el café. A mí me gusta el té.

Now that you know how to correctly use the verb gustar, here is a list of verbs that operate in the same manner:

aburrir
  to bore
fascinar
  to be fascinating to

bastar
    to be sufficient
importar
    to be important to
caer bien (mal)
    to (not) suit
interesar
    to be interesting to
dar asco
    to be loathsome
molestar
    to be a bother
disgustar
    to hate something
parecer
    to appear to be
doler (o:ue)
    to be painful
picar
    to itch
encantar
    to "love" something
quedar
    to be left over, remain
faltar
    to be lacking something
volver (o:ue) loco
    to be crazy about

PRÁCTICA

Select the correct form of gustar

1. Me_____ la comida.
I like the food.

2. Me_____ los libros.
I like the books.

3. Te_____ las pinturas.
You like the paintings.

4. Le_____ la carne.
She likes meat.

B. Select the correct form of faltar.

5. Me_____ el dinero para comprar el anillo.
I'm lacking the money to buy the ring.

6. Nos_____el dinero para comprar los boletos.
We're lacking the money to buy the tickets.

7. Le_____cuatro sillas.
She's lacking four chairs.

8. Le_____el botón.
He's missing a button.

C. Select the correct form of disgustar.

9. Me_____la música moderna.
I hate modern music.

10. Les_____los deportes.
They hate sports.

11. Les_____la televisión.
They hate television.

12. Te_____este libro.
You hate this book.

D. Select the correct form of parecer.

13. La película me_____buena.
The movie seems good to me.

14. Los autos les_____baratos.
The cars seem inexpensive to them.

15. La casa nos_____cara.
The house seems expensive to us.

16. La ropa te_____fea.
The clothing seems ugly to you.

E. Select the correct form of molestar.

17. El ruido les_____mucho.
The noise bothers them a lot.

18. A veces la humedad le_____.
Sometimes, the humidity bothers her.

19. Los anuncios le_____poco.
The commercials bother him little.

CAPÍTULO CATORCE:
REFLEXIVE VERBS

Verbs that indicate that the subject of the sentence does something to himself or herself are called *reflexive.*

In English, reflexive pronouns end in *-self (-selves)*...
I cut myself shaving.
She looked at herself in the mirror.
We embarassed ourselves.
The small children dressed themselves.

Spanish has reflexive pronouns and often uses them in phrases where English does not. The reflexive pronoun still refers back to the subject of the sentence.
  Me levanté a las seis.   *I got up at six.*
  Se lava los dientes.   *He brushes his teeth.*
  Nos vamos.   *Let's go.*

The reflexive pronouns in Spanish are somewhat like the indirect object pronouns. Instead of *le* and *les*, however, the reflexive pronoun *se* is used. The pronoun is placed in front of the verb, and the verb is conjugated for the subject. Here is an example of the conjugated reflexive verb "lavarse", which means "to wash oneself":

(yo) **me** lavo   (nososotros) **nos** lavamos
(tú) **te** lavas   (vosotros) **os** lavais
(el, ella, ud.) **se** lava   (ellos, ellas, uds.) **se** lavan

Ejemplos:

Levantarse temprano.
Yo ___Me___ levanto temprano.
Tú ___Te___ levantas temprano.
Pablo ___Se___ levanta temprano.
Nosotros ___Nos___ levantamos temprano.
Ustedes ___Se___ levantan temprano.
Ana y Lupe ___Se___ levantan temprano.

Acostarse (o-ue) tarde.
Yo ___me___ acuesto tarde.
Tú ___te___ acuestas tarde.
Pablo ___se___ acuesta tarde.
Nosotros ___nos___ acostamos tarde.
Ustedes ___se___ acuestan tarde.
Ana y Lupe ___se___ acuestan tarde

Reflexive pronouns normally are placed directly before the verb, but they may be (but do not have to be) attached to infinitives and present participles.

Me lavo los dientes.
Estoy lavándo<u>me</u> los dientes.
Voy a lavar<u>me</u> los dientes pronto.

PRÁCTICA

Write the reflexive pronoun and the correct form of the verb. Careful! There are some stem-changing verbs.

1. Maria washes her hair. (lavarse)

María _____ _____ el pelo.

2. We take a shower. (ducharse)

Nososotros _____ _____ .

3. They brush their teeth. (cepillarse)

Ellos _____ _____ los dientes.

4. I shave my legs. (afeitarse)

Yo _____ _____ las piernas.

5. The boys fall asleep. (dormirse o:ue)

Los niños _____ _____ .

6. The young ladies get dressed. (vestirse e:i)

Las señoritas _____ _____ .

7. We sit down. (sentarse e:ie) Careful!

Nosotros _____ _____ .

8. Every day I put on makeup. (maquillarse)

Todos los días yo _____ _____ .

CAPÍTULO QUINCE:

SABER VS CONOCER
PEDIR VS PREGUNTAR

In Spanish, there are two verbs that express the idea "to know." These two verbs are "saber" and "conocer." The verb you choose depends upon the context in which it is used. These verbs are **not** interchangeable. Both verbs have irregular "yo" forms (saber – yo sé, conocer – yo conozco). The other 5 forms are regular; they follow the regular "–er" pattern.

To express knowledge or ignorance of a fact or information about something, use "saber."

Juan <u>sabe</u> donde está María.
Juan knows where Maria is.

Yo no <u>sé</u> tu número de teléfono.
I don't know your telephone number.

To say that one is or is not acquainted with a person, a place, or an object, use conocer.

Yo no <u>conozco</u> a María.
I don't know (am not acquainted with) Maria.

Alberto y Alfredo <u>conocen</u> Madrid.
Alberto and Alfredo know (are acquainted with) Madrid.

To express knowledge or ignorance of a subject or learning discipline, use saber or conocer, depending upon the context.

Juan no <u>sabe</u> nada de inglés.
Juan doesn't know any English.

Él <u>sabe</u> matemáticas.
He knows mathematics.

Juan <u>conoce</u> la literatura española.
Juan is familiar with Spanish literature.

To express knowledge or ignorance of a skill, or how to do something, use saber + infinitive.

María <u>sabe conducir</u>.
Maria knows how to drive.

No <u>sé nadar</u> muy bien.
I don't know how to swim very well.

CAPÍTULO QUINCE

To say that you know something by heart, use saber.

María sabe los verbos irregulares.
Maria knows the irregular verbs (by heart).

Ella no sabe la letra de esa canción.
She doesn't know the words to that song.

The situation with regards to the correct use of saber and conocer can be summarized as follows:

saber
to know a fact, to know something thoroughly, to know how to do something

conocer
to be acquainted with a person, place, or thing

PRÁCTICA

Fill in the blanks with the correct form of **saber or conocer**.

1. Juan _____ donde está María. (John knows where Mary is.)

2. Yo no _____ tu número de teléfono. (I don't know your number.)

3. Yo no _____ a María. (I don't know Mary.)

4. Alberto y Alfredo _____ Madrid.

5. Juan no _____ nada de inglés. (John doesn't know English.)

6. Él _____ matemáticas. (He knows math.)

7. Juan _____ la literatura española. (John knows Spanish literature.)

8. María _____ conducir. (Mary knows how to drive.)

9. Nosotros _____ nadar muy bien. (We know how to swim vey well.)

Pedir vs. Preguntar

The same sort of situation exists with respect to the two Spanish verbs **pedir** and **preguntar**. They both mean "to ask" but they are not interchangeable. Fortunately, the rules for using them are a bit more straightforward:

Pedir (e-i)
to ask for, or request an object, service or favor (Pedir is a stem-changing verb.)

Pido más carne.
I ask for more meat.

Pedimos ahora.
We order now (ask for service).

Preguntar
to ask a question, or request information

Pregunto qué hora es.
I ask what time it is.

Preguntamos a qué hora sirven la cena.
We ask what time they serve dinner.

PRÁCTICA

Fill in the blanks with the correct form of **preguntar or pedir**.

1. Yo _____ a Juan. Él sabe los resultados.
I'm asking Juan. He knows the results.

2. Vamos a _____ el dinero.
We are going to ask for the money.

3. Juan_____ más comida.
Juan asks for more food.

4. Voy a_____ a qué hora cierran las puertas.
I'm going to ask what time they close the doors.

5. Los niños siempre_____ regalos.
The children always ask for presents.

6. María_____ cuándo empieza la fiesta.
Maria asks when the party begins.

7. El chico le_____ a la chica para su número de teléfono.
The boy asks the girl for her telephone number.

CAPÍTULO DIECISÉIS GERUNDS

PROGRESSIVE OR "ING" TENSES

Progressive tenses are compound tenses that express actions viewed as being in progress. In English, this tense would be constructed in the following way, the auxiliary verb being "to be".

	TO BE (conjugated)	+	GERUND
present tense	I am	+	running.
past tense	I was	+	running.
future tense	I will be	+	running.

The construction of the Spanish progressive tenses follows the same structure. It's the conjugated auxiliary verb ("estar" = to be) + the gerund

	ESTAR (conjugated)	+	GERUND
present tense	Estoy	+	corriendo.
imperfect tense (past)	Estaba	+	corriendo.
future tense	Estaré	+	corriendo.

Like with English, the progressive tenses in Spanish can be created with any tense (present, past, future, etc.); however, it is most frequently formed with the present and imperfect tenses.

The gerund in Spanish, like in English, gives the progressive tenses their progressive nature. In the English sentence "I am running", running is the gerund; gerunds in English are essentially any words ending in "-ing". Spanish gerunds also have a common ending: "-ndo". Here are a few examples in both English and Spanish.

English gerund (-ing)	Spanish gerund (-ndo)
talking	hablando
walking	caminando
sewing	cosiendo

To form the gerund in Spanish, you remove the infinitive endings (-ar, -er, -ir) and add -ando to the stem of the -ar words and -iendo to the stem of for the -er and -ir verbs. For example:

	infinitive	stem	gerund ending	gerund
-ar verbs	hablar (to talk)	habl-	-ando	hablando (talking)
-er verbs	beber (to drink)	beb-	-iendo	bebiendo (drinking)
-ir verbs	vivir (to live)	viv-	-iendo	viviendo (living)

IRREGULAR PARTICIPLES:

Some participles are irregular and must be memorized:

Ir (to go) – **yendo**
Leer (to read) – **leyendo**
Creer (to think/believe) – **creyendo**

Also, **stem-changing –ir verbs** (like preferir, dormir, vestir, etc) also have a spelling change in their participle.

PRÁCTICA

Tell what the following people are doing right now using the present progressive.

1. Gregorio y yo/estudiar

   _____

2. Tú/ jugar con los chicos

   _____

3. Dolores/escuchar música

   _____

4. Marcos y Rafeal/ leer una novela

   _____

5. Yo/ montar en bicicleta (ride a bike)

   _____

In the following sentences, change the verbs from the present tense to the **present progressive.**

1. Los pasejeros (passengers) miran la película (movie).

   _____

2. Tú y yo preparamos la comida. (food)

   _____

3. Ustedes hacen la tarea. (homework)

   _____

4. Tú comes en la cafetería.

   _____

5. Mi tío (uncle) escribe una carta (a letter).

   _____

CAPÍTULO DIECISIETE: PRETÉRITO/IMPERFECTO

EL PRETÉRITO

To conjugate regular -ar verbs in the preterite (past tense) simply drop the ending (-ar) and add one of the following:

-é
-aste
-ó
-amos
-astéis
-aron

To conjugate regular -er and -ir verbs in the preterite simply drop the ending (-er or -ir) and add one of the following:

-í
-iste
-ió
-imos
-istéis
-ieron

Here are all three regular preterite verb forms together:

hablar	comer	vivir
hablé	comí	viví
hablaste	comiste	viviste
habló	comió	vivió
hablamos	comimos	vivimos
hablastéis	comistéis	vivistéis
hablaron	comieron	vivieron

The nosotros forms for -ar and -ir verbs are the same in both preterite and present tenses: **hablamos, vivimos.**

The preterite is used for actions that can be viewed as single events.

Ella caminó por el parque.
She walked through the park.

Ellos llegaron a las ocho.
They arrived at eight o'clock.

The preterite is used for actions that were repeated a specific number of times, or occurred during a specific period of time.

Ayer escribí tres cartas.
Yesterday I wrote three letters.

Vivimos allí por cuatro años.
We lived there for four years.

The preterite is used for actions that were part of a chain of events.

Ella se levantó, se vistió, y salió de la casa.
She got up, dressed, and left the house.

The preterite is used to state the beginning or the end of an action.

Empezó a nevar a las ocho de la mañana.
It began to snow at eight in the morning.

The above examples all fall within our general rule for using the preterite:

The preterite is used for past actions that are seen as completed.

These are four common irregular verbs in the preterite; you must memorize them:

Ser – to be	Ir – to go	Dar – to give	Hacer – to do/make
fui	fui	Di	hice
fuiste	fuiste	Diste	hiciste
fue	fue	Dio	hizo
fuimos	fuimos	Dimos	hicimos
fuisteis	fuisteis	Disteis	hicisteis
fueron	fueron	Dieron	hicieron

This is not a typo; ser and ir do have identical conjugations in the preterite!

To review some of the rules for using the preterite:

- The preterite is used for actions that can be viewed as single events.
- The preterite is used for actions that were repeated a specific number of times.
- The preterite is used for actions that occurred during a specific period of time.
- The preterite is used for actions that were part of a chain of events.
- The preterite is used to state the beginning or the end of an action.

Verbs (ar,er) that change their stem in the present tense **do not** change in the preterite. They are conjugated just like other regular preterite verbs.

Present	Preterite
entender	**entender**
ent**ie**ndo	entendí
ent**ie**ndes	entendiste
ent**ie**nde	entendió
entendemos	entendimos
entendéis	entendisteis
ent**ie**nden	entendieron

Present	Preterite
cerrar	**cerrar**
c**ie**rro	cerré
c**ie**rras	cerraste
c**ie**rra	cerró
cerramos	cerramos
cerráis	cerrasteis
c**ie**rran	cerraron

Verbs ending in -ir that change their stem in the present tense **do** change in the preterite, but in a different way. They change e:i and o:u in the third person, singular and plural.

Present	Preterite
preferir	**preferir**
pref**ie**ro	preferí
pref**ie**res	preferiste
pref**ie**re	pref**i**rió
preferimos	preferimos
preferís	preferisteis
pref**ie**ren	pref**i**rieron

Present	Preterite
dormir	**dormir**
d**ue**rmo	dormí
d**ue**rmes	dormiste
d**ue**rme	d**u**rmió
dormimos	dormimos
dormís	dormisteis
d**ue**rmen	d**u**rmieron

The following verbs are also irregular in the preterite and must be memorized:

decir	traer	ver
dije	traje	vi
dijiste	trajiste	viste
dijo	trajo	vio
dijimos	trajimos	vimos
dijisteis	trajisteis	visteis
dijeron	trajeron	vieron

Also like traer:

atraer
detraer
distraer
extraer
maltraer
retraer
sustraer

Verbs that end in **-ucir** are irregular and conjugated as follows:

producir

produ**je**
produ**jiste**
produ**jo**
produ**jimos**
produ**jisteis**
produ**jeron**

Other verbs in this category include:

aducir
conducir
coproducir
deducir
inducir
introducir
reducir
traducir

A number of verbs that are irregular in the preterite follow a particular pattern. While their stems change, they all take the following endings:

-e
-iste

-o
-imos
-isteis
-ieron

Here are the verbs, along with their corresponding stem changes:

Infinitive	Stem Change
andar	anduv-
estar	estuv-
tener	tuv-
caber	cup-
haber	hub-
poder	pud-
poner	pus-
saber	sup-
hacer	hic-
querer	quis-
venir	vin-

Here are two examples of how this pattern is applied:

estar (estuv-)	saber (sup-)
estuve	supe
estuviste	supiste
estuvo	supo
estuvimos	supimos
estuvisteis	supisteis
estuvieron	supieron

The one exception is the third person singular of hacer, the c changes to z to form "hizo."

PRÁCTICA

Fill in the blanks with the correct form of the verb in the preterite.

1. Todos los vuelos (flights) _____ (salir) tarde.

2. Yo _____ (mirar) el programa anoche.

3. Los estudiantes _____ (escribir) la tarea.

4. Nosotros _____ (beber) el agua.

5. Ana _____ (escuchar) al profesor.

6. Tú _____ (comer) mucho.

7. Los alumnos _____ (llegar) tarde a clase.

8. Yo _____ (subir) en el telesilla.

9. Ellos _____ (perder) el partido.

10. Enrique _____ (vender) su carro.

11. Nosotros _____ (tomar) la medicina.

12. ¿_____ (estudiar) ustedes la lección?

Combine y escribe una oración. (Combine and write a sentence in the preterite.)

1. Nosotros /tener/que volver a la escuela

2. Ella/ venir/ a comer.

3. Todos/estar/en California de vacación.

4. Tú/saber/de las reglas nuevas.

5. Ella/saber/que el/hacer/ un viaje.

6. Dolores/ir/a buscar su novio

7. mis hermanas me/ver/ bailar.

8. La fiesta/ser/divertida.

9. Antonio y yo / dar/ una fiesta.

10. Mi mamá me/ dar/ muchas cosas para llevar.

Fill in the blanks with the verb in the preterite.

1. Ellos _____ (estar) contentos.

2. Juan y yo _____ (hacer) un pastel.

3. Tu no _____ (poder) ir al cine.

4. Yo _____ (querer) ir a comer pizza.

5. Ud. se _____ (poner) lentes de sol.

6. Juanita _____ (hacer) tarea en cinco minutos.

Make a sentence with the verb and the thing across from it. Combine each line and conjugate the underlined verbs in the preterite.

Tú sacar	una buena nota.
Yo llegar	al café a las dos.
Los chicos	buscar libros en la biblioteca.
Alas once yo empezar	a estudiar
Anoche yo sacar	la basura.
Susi tu ser	la mejor actriz.
Invitir a Jose pero no lo	ver en el concierto
Nosotros praticar	baloncesto ayer
Anteayer yo tocar	la guitarra para mis amigos.
Yo llegar	tarde a la fiesta.
Yo lanzar	la pelota.
Yo pagar	la cuenta
Ustedes sacar	la basura.

El Imperfecto

The imperfect tense is another Spanish past tense, and is used for actions which were:

- **continuous**, or **progressive**, in the past, but which are not complete or may not have been completed.

- It is used for actions that were happening at the same time as another. It is also used for actions in the past that might have been a habitual type of action.

- It can also be used for words ending in -ED, and also for concepts such as "I WAS DOING something when you walked in."

- The Spanish imperfect tense is also used to describe mental, physical states and . . .

- the imperfect tense is used to tell the time in the past . . .

- Regular forms of the imperfect are formed by adding the following endings to the stem of the verb:

-ar verbs example: hablar

aba	hablaba
abas	hablabas
aba	hablaba
ábamos	hablábamos
abais	hablabais
aban	hablaban

-er verbs, -ir verbs	example: vivir
ía	vivía
ías	vivías
ía	vivía
íamos	vivíamos
íais	vivíais
ían	vivían

Only three verbs are irregular in the imperfect:

ser	ver	ir
era	veía	iba
eras	veías	ibas
era	veía	iba
éramos	veíamos	íbamos
erais	veíais	ibais
eran	veían	iban

The uses of the imperfect can be summarized as follows:

Appearance	Victoria era alta y fuerte
Age	Tenía dieciséis Anos
Physical Condition	Estaba cansada
Emocional state	Estaba muy contenta
Attitudes and desires	Ella quería ganar el campeonato
Location	Todos los equipos estaban en la cancha
Date	Era el ocho de octubre
Time	Eran las cuatro de la tarde
Weather	Hacía un poco frio

The imperfect is frequently associated with phrases that describe the frequency of past actions.

a menudo
often

a veces
sometimes

cada día
every day

cada año
every year

con frecuencia
frequently

de vez en cuando
from time to time

en aquella época
at that time

frecuentemente
frequently

generalmente
usually

muchas veces
many times

mucho
a lot

nunca
never

por un rato
for awhile

siempre
always

tantas veces
so many times

todos los días
every day

todo el tiempo
all the time

varias veces
several times

CAPÍTULO DIECISIETE

PRÁCTICA

Fill in the blanks with the indicated verb in the imperfect tense.

1. estudiar --

   A veces los alumnos_____antes de los exámenes.

2. llamar --

   El muchacho frecuentemente le_____a la muchacha a las diez de la noche.

3. llamar --

   Ud. frecuentemente me_____antes de las nueve de la mañana.

4. estar --

   Todo el día la alumna_____en la universidad.

5. estar --

   Todo el día yo_____en la casa.

6. comer --

   Nosotros_____en este restaurante con frecuencia

7. ser –

   _____las tres de la tarde.

8. estar --

   Todo el día tú_____en el edificio.

9. llamar --

   La muchacha nunca le_____al muchacho antes de las ocho de la noche.

10. limpiar --

    Usted_____el coche cada semana.

11. poder --

    Tú_____ayudarme.

12. escribir --

    A menudo ellos_____libros importantes.

13. estar --

    Yo nunca_____feliz.

14. estudiar --

    María siempre_____antes de una prueba.

15. vivir --

    Carmen y José_____en la América Central cuando yo me casé.

16. ver --

    Tú_____a María en la cama.

17. ver --

    Los chicos_____a las chicas en el jardín.

18. estar --

    Los niños nunca_____preocupados.

19. ir --

    Yo_____a la playa con frecuencia.

20. ir --

    El muchacho_____a la escuela cada día.

CAPÍTULO DIECIOCHO: FUTURE AND CONDITIONAL TENSES

El Futuro

The future tense is used to tell what "will" happen, or what "shall" happen.

I **will** go to the beach next month.
I **shall** write the letter next week.

But, the future tense is **not** used to express a willingness to do something. For this, use the verb "querer."

¿Quieres ir a la tienda?
Will you go to the store?

The future tense is also used to express wonder or probability in the present state.

¿Quién será ella?
I wonder who she is? (Who could she be?)

Estará viajando solo.
He is probably traveling alone.

For actions that will occur in the near future, the present tense is more commonly used.

Esta noche voy al cine.
Tonight I'm going to the movies.

Further in the future, use the future tense.

El año que viene iré a España.
Next year I'm going to Spain.

All regular verbs in the future tense are conjugated by adding the following endings to the infinitive form of the verb: **-é, -ás, -á, -emos, -éis, -án**.

hablaré
hablarás
hablará
hablaremos
hablaréis
hablarán

There are twelve common verbs that are irregular in the future tense. Their endings are regular, but their stems change. Since the endings are the same as all other future tense verbs, we show only the "yo" form, and have underlined the irregular stem. We have also grouped them according to their patterns of change.

caber
yo cabré

poner
yo pondré

decir
yo diré

haber
yo habré

salir
yo saldré

hacer
yo haré

poder
yo podré

tener
yo tendré

querer
yo querré

valer
yo valdré

saber
yo sabré

venir
yo vendré

PRÁCTICA
Fill in the blanks with the correct form of the future tense.

1. Nosotros _____ estudiar para el examen. (tener).
2. Los estudiantes _____ de Madrid a las ocho. (salir)
3. Ellas _____ a la fiesta con Ramón mañana. (ir)

4. ¿Le _____ tú nuestros planes a Miguel? (decir)
5. Ellos no _____ ir el viernes. (poder)
6. Yo no _____ la tarea hoy. (hacer)
7. Elena no _____ viajar. (querer)
8. Uds. _____ temprano. (despertarse) Careful!
9. Los ciclistas no _____ nada. (saber)
10. Yo no _____ hasta muy tarde. (levantarse)
11. El profesor no _____ los verbos en el examen. (poner)
12. Ud. _____ lo que sea. (decir)
13. Yo _____ (ir) a España este verano.
14. Nosotros _____ (asistir) la fiesta el viernes que viene.
15. En el futuro yo _____ (ser) mas alto.
16. ¿_____ (estar) tú en la biblioteca?
17. Luego ellos _____ (preparar) la cena.
18. El año que viene ella _____ (sacar) buenas notas.

The Conditional Tense

Frequently, the conditional is used to express probability, possibility, wonder or conjecture and is usually translated as would, could, must have or probably.

The student said that he <u>would study</u> one more hour. (probability, possibility)
What time <u>could</u> it <u>have been</u>? (wonder, conjecture)
He <u>must have been</u> at home. (wonder, conjecture)
We <u>were probably</u> busy when you called. (probability, possibility)

Note: when "would" is used in the sense of a repeated action in the past, the imperfect is used.

To conjugate regular -ar, -er and -ir verbs in the conditional, simply add one of the following to the infintive:

ía
ías
ía
íamos
íais

ían

Here are all three regular conditional verb forms together:

hablar	**comer**	**vivir**
hablaría	comería	viviría
hablarías	comerías	vivirías
hablaría	comería	viviría
hablaríamos	comeríamos	viviríamos
hablaríais	comeríais	viviríais
hablarían	comerían	vivirían

Here are the previous examples, translated to Spanish.

El alumno dijo que estudiaría una hora más.
The student said that he would study one more hour.

¿Qué hora sería?
What time could it have been?

Estaría en su casa.
He must have been at home.

Estaríamos ocupados cuando llamaste.
We were probably busy when you called.

The same twelve common verbs that are irregular in the future tense are also irregular in the conditional tense. Their endings are regular, but their stems change in the same way they change in the future tense. Because the endings are the same as all other conditional tense verbs, we show only the "yo" form, and have underlined the irregular stem. We have also grouped them according to their patterns of change.

caber
yo <u>cabr</u>ía

poner
yo <u>pondr</u>ía

decir
yo <u>dir</u>ía

haber
yo <u>habr</u>ía

salir
yo <u>saldr</u>ía

hacer
yo <u>har</u>ía

poder
yo <u>podr</u>ía

tener
yo <u>tendr</u>ía

querer
yo <u>querr</u>ía

valer
yo <u>valdr</u>ía

saber
yo <u>sabr</u>ía

venir
yo <u>vendr</u>ía

Here are some specific uses of the conditional tense:

To express speculation about the past:
    Aquél día correrían más de veinticinco kilómetros.
    That day they must have run more than 25 kilometers.
To express the future from the perspective of the past:
    Yo sabía que abrirían la tienda a las siete.
    I knew that they would open the store at seven o'clock.
To express hypothetical actions or events which may or may not occur:
    Sería interesante estudiar chino.
    It would be interesting to study Chinese.
To indicate what would happen were it not for some certain specific circumstance:
    Yo viajaría pero no tengo dinero.
    I would travel but I don't have money.
For polite use to soften requests:
    Por favor, ¿podría decirme a qué hora abre la gasolinera?
    Could you please tell me what time the gas station opens?
To ask for advice:
    ¿Cuál compraría Ud.?
    Which one would you buy?
For reported speech:
    Juan dijo que terminaría el trabajo.

Juan said that he would finish the work.
To express what would be done in a particular situation:
¿Hablarías inglés en España?
Would you speak English in Spain?
No. Hablaría español.
No. I would speak Spanish.

PRÁCTICA

Fill in the blanks with the verb in the conditional tense.

1. Rodrigo _____ una casa en las montañas, pero no le gusta la nieve. (Comprar)

2. Yo _____ la papas fritas pero no tengo hambre. (Comer)

3. Paco y Ana _____ en las montañas pero están enfermos. (esquiar)

4. Ellas _____ una blusa blanca, pero los blue jeans están sucios. (Llevar)

5. El Sr. Smith_____ ahora, pero no puede. (Salir)

6. Nosotros_____ la tarea, pero no tenemos un libro. (Hacer)

7. ¿_____ tú a la playa o al cine? (Ir)

8. Ustedes _____ ir al cine, pero tienen que hacer la tarea. (Poder)

9. El profesor _____ la palabra correcta pero tiene laryngitis. (Decir)

10. Luis _____ la carpeta en su mochila, pero no la tiene.

(Poner)

11. Cecilia y tú _____ a España pero no tienen dinero. (ir)

12. La casa de mi abuela _____ muy grande, pero no le gusta limpiar. (ser)

13. Usted _____ a otro pais pero no tiene pasaporte. (Visitar)

14. Mis hermanos _____ otro carro nuevo, pero cuesta demasiado. (querer)

CAPÍTULO DIECINUEVE: PRESENT PERFECT/PAST PERFECT

The Present Perfect

The present perfect is formed by combining the auxiliary verb "has" or "have" with the past participle.

I <u>have studied</u>.
He <u>has written</u> a letter to María.
We <u>have been</u> stranded for six days.

Because the present perfect is a compound tense, two verbs are required: the *main* verb and the *auxiliary* verb.

I have studied.
(main verb: studied ; auxiliary verb: have)

He has written a letter to María.
(main verb: written ; auxiliary verb: has)

We have been stranded for six days.
(main verb: been ; auxiliary verb: have)

In Spanish, the present perfect tense is formed by using the present tense of the auxiliary verb "haber" with the past participle. Haber is conjugated as follows:

he	hemos
has	habéis
ha	han

You have already learned in a previous lesson that the past participle is formed by dropping the infinitive ending and adding either -ado or -ido. Remember, some past participles are irregular. The following examples all use the past participle for the verb "comer."

(yo) **He comido.**
I have eaten.

(tú) **Has comido.**
You have eaten.

(él) **Ha comido.**
He has eaten.

(nosotros) **Hemos comido.**
We have eaten.

(vosotros) **Habéis comido.**

You-all have eaten.

(ellos) **Han comido.**
They have eaten.

When you studied the past participle, you practiced using it as an adjective. When used as an adjective, the past participle changes to agree with the noun it modifies. However, when used in the perfect tenses, the past participle never changes.

Past participle used as an adjective:
La cuenta está pagada.
The bill is paid.

Past participle used in the present perfect tense:
He pagado la cuenta.
I have paid the bill.

Here's a couple of more examples:

Past participle used as an adjective:
Las cuentas están pagadas.
The bills are paid.

Past participle used in the present perfect tense:
Juan ha pagado las cuentas.
Juan has paid the bills.

Note that when used to form the present perfect tense, only the base form (pagado) is used.

Let's look more carefully at the last example:

Juan ha pagado las cuentas.
Juan has paid the bills.

Notice that we use "ha" to agree with "Juan". We do not use "han" to agree with "cuentas." The auxiliary verb is conjugated for the subject of the sentence, not the object. Compare these two examples:

Juan ha pagado las cuentas.
Juan has paid the bills.

Juan y María han viajado a España.
Juan and Maria have traveled to Spain.

In the first example, we use "ha" because the subject of the sentence is "Juan." In the second example, we use "han" because the subject of the sentence is "Juan y María."

The present perfect tense is frequently used for past actions that continue into the present, or continue to affect the present.

He estado dos semanas en Madrid.
I have been in Madrid for two weeks.

Diego ha sido mi amigo por veinte años.
Diego has been my friend for 20 years.

The present perfect tense is often used with the adverb "ya".

Ya han comido.
They have already eaten.

La empleada ya ha limpiado la casa.
The maid has already cleaned the house.

The auxiliary verb and the past participle are never separated. To make the sentence negative, add the word "no" *before* the conjugated form of haber.

(Yo) **No he comido.**
I have not eaten.

(Tú) **No has comido.**
You have not eaten.

(Él) **No ha comido.**
He has not eaten.

(Nosotros) **No hemos comido.**
We have not eaten.

(Vosotros) **No habéis comido.**
You-all have not eaten.

(Ellos) **No han comido.**
They have not eaten.

Again, the auxiliary verb and the past participle are <u>never</u> separated. Object pronouns are placed immediately before the auxiliary verb.

Pablo le ha dado mucho dinero a su hermana.
Pablo has given a lot of money to his sister.

To make this sentence negative, "no" is placed before the indirect object pronoun (le).

Pablo no le ha dado mucho dinero a su hermana.
Pablo has not given a lot of money to his sister.

With reflexive verbs, the reflexive pronoun is placed immediatedly before the auxiliary verb. Compare how the present perfect differs from the simple present when a reflexive verb is used.

Me cepillo los dientes. (present)
I brush my teeth.

Me he cepillado los dientes. (present perfect)
I have brushed my teeth.

To make this sentence negative, the word "no" is placed before the reflexive pronoun (me).

No me he cepillado los dientes.
I have not brushed my teeth.

Questions are formed as follows. Note how the word order is different than the English equivalent.

¿Han salido ya las mujeres?
Have the women left yet?

¿Has probado el chocolate alguna vez?
Have you ever tried chocolate?

Here are the same sentences in negative form. Notice how the auxiliary verb and the past participle are not separated.

¿No han salido ya las mujeres?
Haven't the women left yet?

¿No has probado el chocolate ninguna vez?
Haven't you ever tried chocolate?

PRÁCTICA
Translate using the present perfect.

1. you (tú) have lived
   _____

2. Juan has eaten
   _____

3. we have studied
   _____

4. you-all (vosotros) have seen
   _____

5. you-all (ustedes) have spoken
   _____

6. they have left
   _____

7. Juan and Maria have been
   _____

8. I have drank
   _____

9. we have listened to
   _____

10. she has washed
    _____

The Past Perfect

The past perfect is formed by combining the auxiliary verb "had" with the past participle.

I <u>had studied</u>.
He <u>had written</u> a letter to María.
We <u>had been</u> stranded for six days.

Because the past perfect is a compound tense, two verbs are required: the *main* verb and the *auxiliary* verb.

I had studied.
(main verb: studied ; auxiliary verb: had)

He had written a letter to María.
(main verb: written ; auxiliary verb: had)

We had been stranded for six days.
(main verb: been ; auxiliary verb: had)

In Spanish, the past perfect tense is formed by using the imperfect tense of the auxiliary verb "haber" with the past participle. Haber is conjugated as follows:

había	habíamos
habías	habíais
había	habían

You have already learned in a previous lesson that the past participle is formed by dropping the infinitive ending and adding either -ado or -ido. Remember, some past participles are irregular. The following examples all use the past participle for the verb "vivir."

(yo) **Había vivido.**
I had lived.

(tú) **Habías vivido.**
You had lived.

(él) **Había vivido.**
He had lived.

(nosotros) **Habíamos vivido.**
We had lived.

(vosotros) **Habíais vivido.**
You-all had lived.

(ellos) **Habían vivido.**
They had lived.

When you studied the past participle, you practiced using it as an adjective. When used as an adjective, the past participle changes to agree with the noun it modifies. However, when used in the perfect tenses, the past participle never changes.

Past participle used as an adjective:
La puerta está cerrada.
The door is closed.

Past participle used in the past perfect tense:
Yo había cerrado la puerta.
I had closed the door.

Here are a couple of more examples:

Past participle used as an adjective:
Las puertas están abiertas.
The doors are open.

Past participle used in the past perfect tense:
Juan había abierto las puertas.
Juan had opened the doors.

Note that when used to form the perfect tenses, only the base form (abierto) is used.

Let's look more carefully at the last example:

Juan había abierto las puertas.
Juan had opened the doors.

Notice that we use "había" to agree with "Juan". We do NOT use "habían" to agree with "puertas." The auxiliary verb is conjugated for the subject of the sentence, not the object. Compare these two examples:

Juan había abierto las puertas.
Juan had opened the doors.

Juan y María habían puesto mucho dinero en el banco.
Juan and Maria had put a lot of money in the bank.

In the first example, we use "había" because the subject of the sentence is "Juan." In the second example, we use "habían" because the subject of the sentence is "Juan y María."

The past perfect tense is used when a past action was completed prior to another past action. Expressions such as "ya", "antes", "nunca", "todavía" and "después" will often appear in sentences where one action was completed before another.

Cuando llegaron los padres, los niños ya habían comido.
When the parents arrived, the children had already eaten.

Yo había comido antes de llamarles.
I had eaten prior to calling them.

This idea of a past action being completed before another past action need not always be stated; it can be implied.

Juan había cerrado la ventana antes de salir. (stated)
Juan had closed the window before leaving.

Juan había cerrado la ventana. (implied)
Juan had closed the window.

The auxiliary verb and the past participle are never separated. To make the sentence negative, add the word "no" *before* the conjugated form of haber.

(yo) **No había vivido.**
I had not lived.

(tú) **No habías vivido.**
You had not lived.

(él) **No había vivido.**
He had not lived.

(nosotros) **No habíamos vivido.**
We had not lived.

(vosotros) **No <u>habíais vivido</u>.**
You-all had not lived.

(ellos) **No <u>habían vivido</u>.**
They had not lived.

Again, the auxiliary verb and the past participle are <u>never</u> separated. Object pronouns are placed immediately before the auxiliary verb.

Pablo <u>le había dado</u> mucho dinero a su hermana.
Pablo had given a lot of money to his sister.

To make this sentence negative, "no" is placed before the indirect object pronoun (le).

Pablo <u>no le había dado</u> mucho dinero a su hermana.
Pablo had not given a lot of money to his sister.

With reflexive verbs, the reflexive pronoun is placed immediatedly before the auxiliary verb. Compare how the present perfect differs from the simple present, when a reflexive verb is used.

<u>Me lavo</u> las manos. (present)
I wash my hands.

<u>Me había lavado</u> las manos. (past perfect)
I had washed my hands.

To make this sentence negative, the word "no" is placed before the reflexive pronoun (me).

<u>No me había lavado</u> las manos.
I had not washed my hands.

Questions are formed as follows. Note how the word order is different than the English equivalent.

¿Habían llegado ya las chicas?
Had the girls arrived yet?

¿Habías probado ya el postre?
Had you tried the dessert yet?

Here are the same questions in negative form. Notice how the auxiliary verb and the past participle are not separated.

¿No habían llegado ya las chicas?
Hadn't the girls arrived yet?

¿No habías probado ya el postre?
Hadn't you tried the dessert yet?

PRÁCTICA

Circle the correct answer.

1. Carlos _____ corrido en la playa. (había, haber, habían)

2. Nosotros habíamos _____ con el director. (hablar, hablado, habló)

3. Yo _____ lavado las toallas. (habían, habíamos, había)

4. Rosa había _____ ajedrez. (jugó, jugado, jugar)

5. Tú _____ soñado con un ángel. (habías, haber, hubo)

6. Esas aves habían _____ a la laguna. (volado, volar, volando)

7. Pedro y Juan _____ jugado con el perro. (habían, había, habías)

8. Yo había _____ un pastel con cerezos. (cocinar, cocina, cocinado)

9. Ella _____ volado en avión con mamá. (habíamos, había, haber)

10. Tú habías _____ con Mario por teléfono. (hablado, hablar, hablando)

11. Él _____ nadado en el lago. (había, habíamos, habían)

12. Nosotros _____ vendido las blusas. (habíamos, haber, habían)

CAPÍTULO VEINTE: COMMANDS AND SUBJUNCTIVE

Formal Commands

Commands are used when ordering, or telling someone to do something. This is often referred to as the "imperative" form of the verb.

Compre Ud. el anillo.
    (You) Buy the ring.
Haga Ud. la tarea.
    (You) Do the homework.
Compren Uds. los libros.
    (You-all) Buy the books.
Hagan Uds. el trabajo.
    (You-all) Do the work.

By now, you are well acquainted with the fact that Spanish has both a formal and an informal style of speech (tú / Ud.). This distinction applies to commands.

Compre Ud. el anillo.
    Buy the ring. (formal)
Compra (tú) los dulces.
    Buy the candy. (familiar)

Informal, or familiar, speech is used among friends, coworkers, relatives, or when addressing a child. Formal speech is generally used to be polite or to express respect. For that reason, the formal commands are often referred to as **polite commands**.

The formal commands are formed the same way as the present subjunctive:

1. Start with the **yo** form of the present indicative.
2. Then drop the **-o** ending.
3. Finally, add the following endings:

-ar verbs:
-e (for Ud.), -en (for Uds.)

-er and -ir verbs:
-a (for Ud.), -an (for Uds.)

The following examples of formal commands use three regular verbs: hablar, comer, and escribir.

Hable Ud. más lentamente.
Hablen Uds. más lentamente.
Speak more slowly.

Coma Ud. la cena.
Coman Uds. la cena.
Eat the dinner.

Escriba Ud. la carta.
Escriban Uds. la carta.
Write the letter.

Remember, if the first person singular (yo) form is irregular, that irregularity is carried over into the formation of the formal command.

Tengan Uds. un buen viaje. (yo tengo)
Have a good trip.
Traiga Ud. el dinero. (yo traigo)
Bring the money.
Venga Ud. conmigo. (yo vengo)
Come with me.

This also applies to stem-changing verbs.

Cuente Ud. sus beneficios. (yo cuento)
Count your blessings.
Vuelvan Uds. pronto. (yo vuelvo)
Return quickly.
Pida dinero. (yo pido)
Ask for money.

As with the present subjunctive, the following verbs have irregular command forms:

dar
dé Ud.
den Uds.

estar
esté Ud.
estén Uds.

ir
vaya Ud.
vayan Uds.

ser
sea Ud.
sean Uds.

saber

sepa Ud.
sepan Uds.

Note that affirmative and negative commands use the same verb forms.

Hable Ud.
Speak.
No hable Ud.
Don't speak.
Coma Ud.
Eat.
No coma Ud.
Don't eat.
Escriba Ud.
Write.
No escriba Ud.
Don't write.

Also note that the subject pronouns Ud. and Uds. may or may not be used. Using them adds a degree of formality or politeness to the command.

Hable
Speak.
Hable Ud.
Speak (sir). (more respectful)
Coma.
Eat.
Coma Ud.
Eat (sir). (more polite)

Informal Commands ("tú")

In the previous lesson, you learned that commands are used when ordering, or telling someone to do something. This is often referred to as the "imperative" form of the verb.

Compra (tú) el anillo.
(You) Buy the ring.

Escribe (tú) la tarea.
(You) Do the homework.

Compra (tú) los libros.
(You) Buy the books.

Come (tú) la patata.
(You) Eat the potato.

Remember that Spanish has both a formal and an informal style of speech (tú/Ud.). This distinction applies to commands.

Compre Ud. el anillo.
Buy the ring. (formal)

Compra (tú) los dulces.
Buy the candy. (familiar)

Remember, formal speech is generally used to be polite or to express respect. Informal, or familiar, speech is used among friends, coworkers, relatives, or when addressing a child.

The affirmative informal (tú) commands are formed the same way as the present indicative Ud. form:

(hablar - ar + a = habla)
(comer - er + e = come)
(escribir - ir + e = escribe)

Be sure to note that the "tú" commands use the <u>usted</u> form, not the tú form!

The following examples of commands use three regular verbs: hablar, comer, and escribir.

Habla (tú) más lentamente.
(You) Speak more slowly.

Come (tú) la cena.
(You) Eat the dinner.

Escribe (tú) la carta.
(You) Write the letter.

Note that the negative informal commands use the tú form of the present subjunctive.

No cuentes tus beneficios.
Don't count your blessings.

No hables más lentamente.
Don't speak more slowly.

Be sure to note that this <u>is</u> the tú form!

Compare the affirmative informal (tú) commands with the negative informal (tú) commands:

Cuenta tus beneficios.
Count your blessings.
No cuentes tus beneficios.
Don't count your blessings.
Habla más lentamente.
Speak more slowly.
No hables más lentamente.
Don't speak more slowly.

Also note that the subject pronoun tú is not normally used with imperative form.

Habla más lentamente.
(You) Speak more slowly.

Come la cena.
(You) Eat the dinner.

Escribe la carta.
(You) Write the letter.

Irregular Commands ("tú")

The following eight verbs have irregular familiar commands in the affirmative:

decir - di   **salir - sal**

hacer - haz   **ser - sé**

ir - ve   **tener - ten**

poner - pon   **venir - ven**

Note that these irregularities only occur with affirmative tú commands. As with all other verbs, to form negative informal commands with these verbs, use the "tú" form of the present subjunctive.

Di la verdad.
(Tell the truth.)
No digas mentiras.
(Don't tell lies.)
Haz tu tarea.
(Do your homework.)

No hagas eso.
(Don't do that.)

First Person Commands ("nosotros")

Nosotros commands are used when the speaker is included, and are used to express the idea "let's + verb." To form these commands, use the nosotros form of the present subjunctive.

Comamos allí.
Let's eat there.

Contemos el dinero.
Let's count the money.

To form the negative command, place the word **no** before the same verb form (present subjunctive).

No comamos allí.
Let's not eat there.

No contemos el dinero.
Let's not count the money.

The only exception is the verb ir(se), which uses the present indicative for the affirmative command only.

<u>**Vamos**</u> **ahora.**
Let's go now.

but

<u>**No vayamos**</u> **a la tienda.**
Let's not go to the store.

As with other commands, a written accent is often required when pronouns are added. With affirmative commands, the final "s" of the verb form is dropped before adding the pronouns "nos" or "se."

Sentemos + nos = Sentémonos.
Let's sit down.

Escribamos + se + la = Escribámosela.
Let's write it to them.

But not with negative commands.

No nos sentemos.
Let's not sit down.

No se la escribamos.
Let's not write it to them.

Note that "Vamos a + infinitive" can also be used to convey the meaning "Let's ___."
Note the two different ways of saying the same thing.

Trabajemos juntos.
Let's work together.

Vamos a trabajar juntos.
Let's work together.

The Subjunctive

All too frequently, the topic of the subjunctive is made far more difficult than is necessary. Let's try a slightly different approach, with the goal of making this topic less troublesome. The subjunctive is not a tense; rather, it is a mood. **Tense** refers to when an action takes place (past, present, future), while **mood** merely reflects how the speaker feels about the action. The subjunctive mood is rarely used in English, but it is widely used in Spanish.

Here are some examples of the subjunctive being used in English:

The doctor recommends that he take the pills with food.
Subjunctive conjugation: he take

The law requires that you be 18 years old to vote.
Subjunctive conjugation: you be

If I were a rich man, I wouldn't have to work hard.
Subjunctive conjugation: I were

So far, you have studied verb tenses in the **indicative** mood. The indicative mood is used to express factual information, certainty, and objectivity.

Usted va al Perú en diciembre.

You are going to Peru in December.

The above sentence merely reports the fact that you are going to Peru in December, so the indicative mood is used.

Let's change the above example slightly:

No dudo que usted **va** al Perú en diciembre.

I don't doubt that you are going to Peru in December.

In the above sentence, the clause "no dudo" introduces a quality of **certainty**, -- the speaker has no doubt, so the indicative mood is used in the second clause **(va)** as well as the first **(no dudo)**.

Let's make another slight change to our example:

Dudo que usted **vaya** al Perú en diciembre.

I doubt that you are going to Peru in December.

In the above sentence, the clause "dudo" introduces a quality of **uncertainty**, -- the speaker does have doubt, so here the subjunctive mood is used in the second clause **(vaya)**. The **subjunctive** mood is used to express everything except certainty and objectivity: things like doubt, uncertainty, subjectivity, etc.

Yo dudo que usted vaya al Perú en diciembre.

I doubt that you are going to Peru in December.

Since the above statement does not express certainty, the subjunctive **(vaya)** is required in the second clause. The difference between indicative and subjunctive is the difference between certainty/objectivity (indicative) and possibility/subjectivity (subjunctive).

Indicative

John goes to the store.
(This sentence merely states the certain, objective fact that John goes to the store.)

I know that John goes to the store.
(The clause "I know" tells us that the speaker feels that it is a certain, objective fact that John goes to the store.)

There is no doubt that John goes to the store.
(The clause "there is no doubt" tells us that the speaker feels that it is a certain, objective fact that John goes to the store.)

Subjunctive

I want John to go to the store.
(The clause "I want" tells us that the speaker feels that there is uncertainty as to whether John goes to the store.)

I hope that John goes to the store.
(The clause "I hope" tells us that the speaker feels that there is uncertainty as to whether John goes to the store.)

It is possible that John will go to the store.
(The clause "it is possible" tells us that the speaker feels that there is uncertainty as to whether John goes to the store.)

It's good that John goes to the store.
(The clause "it's good" alerts us that the speaker is about to express a subjective opinion.)

It's important that John goes to the store.
(The clause "it's important" alerts us that the speaker is about to express a subjective opinion.)

Because there must be some uncertainty or subjectivity to warrant the use of the subjunctive, you will usually see it in sentences that contain a main clause which introduces a quality of uncertainty or subjectivity.

I hope she will come.
I hope = main clause

I know she will come.
I know = main clause

I feel she will come.
I feel = main clause.

The above examples all have main clauses, but only the first and the third introduce an element of uncertainty or subjectivity.

In learning to use the subjunctive, it is quite helpful if one can first recognize such clauses. The following is a list of clauses commonly associated with the use of the subjunctive:

a menos que ...
unless ...

antes (de) que ...
before ...

con tal (de) que ...
provided that ...

cuando ...
when ...

conviene que ...
it is advisable that ...

después (de) que ...
after ...

dudar que ...
to doubt that ...

en caso de que ...
in case ...

en cuanto ...
as soon as ...

es aconsejable que ...
it's advisable that ...

es bueno que ...
it's good that ...

es difícil que ...
it's unlikely that ...

es dudoso que ...
it is doubtful that ...

es fácil que ...
it's likely that ...

es fantástico que ...
it's fantastic that ...

es importante que ...
it's important that ...

es imposible que ...
it's impossible that ...

es improbable que ...
it's unlikely that ...

es incierto que ...
it's uncertain that ...

es increíble que ...
it's incredible that ...

es (una) lástima que ...
it's a pity that ...

es malo que ...
it's bad that ...

es mejor que ...
it's better that ...

es menester que ...
it's necessary that ...

es necesario que ...
it's necessary that ...

esperar que ...
to wish that ...

es posible que ...
it's possible that ...

es preciso que ...
it's necessary that ...

es preferible que ...
it's preferable that ...

es probable que ...
it's probable that ...

es raro que ...
it's rare that ...

es ridículo que ...
it's ridiculous that ...

estar contento que
to be happy that ...

es terrible que ...
it's terrible that ...

hasta que ...
until ...

insistir en que ...
to insist that ...

mandar que ...
to order that ...

más vale que ...
it's better that ...

mientras que ...
while ...

negar que ...
to deny that ...

no creer que ...
not to believe that ...

no es cierto que ...
it's not certain that ...

no estar convencido de que ...
to not be convinced that ...

no estar seguro de que ...
to not be sure that ...

no es verdad que ...
it's not true that ...

no imaginarse que ...
to not imagine that ...

no parecer que ...
to not seem that ...

no pensar que ...
to not think that ...

no suponer que ...
to not suppose that ...

ojalá que ...
if only he would ...

para que ...
in order that ...

pedir que ...
to ask that ...

preferir que ...
to prefer that ...

prohibir que ...
to prohibit that ...

puede ser que ...
it may be that ...

querer que ...
to want that ...

recomendar que ...
to recommend that ...

rogar que ...
to plead that ...

sentir que ...
to regret that ...

sin que ...
without ...

sugerir que ...
to suggest that ...

tan pronto como ...
as soon as ...

temer que ...
to fear that ...

tener miedo de que ...
to be afraid that ...

As you can see, the list is quite long, and this isn't even a complete list! There are even more expressions that trigger use of the subjunctive that we haven't included. Instead of trying to memorize such a long list, why not familiarize yourself with a much shorter list of expressions with which the subjunctive is **not** used?

creer que ...
to believe that ...

no dudar que ...
to not doubt that ...

es cierto que ...
it is certain that ...

es claro que ...
it is clear that ...

es evidente que ...
it is certain that ...

es obvio que ...
it is obvious that ...

estar seguro que ...

to be sure that ...

es verdad que ...
it is true that ...

no cabe duda que ...
there's no doubt that ...

no es dudoso que ...
it is not doubtful that ...

no hay duda que ...
there is no doubt that ...

Since these expressions introduce a quality of **certainty**, they do **not** trigger the use of the subjunctive. If you encounter a sentence with a main clause followed by a second clause, and the main clause introduces a quality of **certainty** or **objectivity**, the sentence will use the **indicative mood** in the second clause, since the sentence will be reporting something certain. If you encounter a sentence with a main clause followed by a second clause, and the main clause does **not** introduce a quality of **certainty** or **objectivity**, the sentence will usually use the **subjunctive mood** in the second clause, since the sentence will **not** be reporting something certain.

CAPÍTULO VEINTIUNO: POR VS PARA

These prepositions are very common in Spanish and, unfortunately, both often correspond to English "for". The following is an attempt to summarize the main uses of the two.

PARA (destination or purpose):

1. Direction toward a destination or goal:

Salgo mañana para Madrid.	I am leaving tomorrow for Madrid.
Vamos para la oficina.	We're going to the office.

2. Purpose, use, goal or destination toward a recipient:

taza para café coffee cup	llantas para la nieve snowtires
Había espacio para todos.	There was room for everybody.
Estudié medicina para ayudar.	I studied medicine in order to help.
Practican para mejorar.	They practice to improve.
Compró estos libros para ti.	He bought these books for you.
Trabaja para la OTAN.	She works for NATO.

3. Time limit or deadline:

Hay que hacerlo para el lunes.	It needs to be done by/for Monday.

4. Comparison against the normal expectation:
Tiene una gran población para un país tan pequeño.
It has a large population for such a small country.
Para ser extranjero, habla muy bien el idioma.
For a foreigner, he speaks the language very well.

5. Opinion: "To me..."

Para mí, la política es interesante.	To me, politics is interesting.
La vida es valiosa para cualquiera.	Life is valuable to anyone.

Use para in Spanish whenever you could use "in order to" in English. For example:

(in order) To improve, people have to do this.	Para mejorar, hay que hacer esto.
I do it (in order) to have fun.	Lo hago para divertirme.
I do it to improve.	Lo hago para mejorar.
BUT:	
It's not easy to improve this.	No es fácil mejorar esto.
(you couldn't insert "in order to" here)	

POR (motivation or substitution):

1. Exchange, substitution, rate, correspondence (per):

Te doy cinco dólares por el libro.	I'll give you five dollars for the book.
Gracias por todo.	Thanks for everything.
No me tomes por idiota.	Don't take me for an idiot.
a veinte kilómetros por hora	twenty kilometers an hour
el diez por ciento	ten percent
$3 por galón.	$3 per gallon

2. a. Cause, reason, or motive of an action (because of, to fetch):

Lo merece por su dedicación.	He deserves it for (because of) his dedication.
Fuimos al mercado por pan.	We went to the store for bread.
Te quería por tu honestidad.	I loved you for your honesty.
No jugaron por la lluvia.	They didn't play because of the rain.

b. On behalf of, for the sake of, in favor of, out of:

Lo hice por el dinero.	I did it for the money.
No lo hago por ti.	I'm not doing it on your account.
Se preocupan por mí.	They worry about me.
Luchan por la independencia.	They fight for independence.
Trabajaba por la paz mundial.	She worked for world peace.
A menudo me pregunta por ti.	He often asks about you.

4. Duration in time (often omitted):

Estuvo en México (por) seis semanas. He was (stayed) in Mexico for six weeks. During the morning, evening, or afternoon: Trabajaba por la mañana. He used to work in the morning.

4. Movement through a place:

Iba por la calle cuando...	I was going down the street...
Pasa por mi oficina.	Drop by my office.
Vamos a pasear por el parque.	We are going to take a walk through/by the park.

5. Agent in a passive phrase (by):

Fue escrito por ella.	It was written by her.
Está afectada por la noticia.	She's affected by the news.

6. Means of transportation or communication (by):

El paquete llegó por avión.	The package arrived by plane.
Llámame por teléfono.	Call me on the telephone.

7. In a large number of idiomatic expressions:

por fin	finally, at last	por lo menos	at least
por ejemplo	for example	por favor	please
por desgracia	unfortunately	por primera vez	for the first time
por supuesto	of course	por casualidad	by (any) chance
por eso	that's why	por otra parte	on the other hand
por aquí	around here	por lo tanto	therefore

The questions ¿para qué? (for what purpose?) and ¿por qué? (for what reason or motive?) can give you clues on choosing the appropriate preposition. Both prepositions will often be grammatically correct, but they would convey different meanings:

Recibimos dinero por la investigación.
I got money from the research (done). [exchange]

Recibimos dinero para la investigación.
I got money for the research (to do). [purpose]

Compré esto por ti.
I bought this because you wanted me to. [motive]

Compré esto para ti.
I bought this to give it to you. [destination]

PRÁCTICA
Decide if you need to use **por or para.**

Decide if you need to use por or para.

1. Elena va a casarse [por, para] amor. (She's going to marry for love.)

2. Elizabeth tiene que hacerlo [por, para] mañana. (She has to do it for tomorrow.)

3. Luisa estudia [por, para] ser médico. (Luisa is studying to be a doctor.)

4. Gracias [por, para] el regalo. (Thanks for the gift.)

5. Yo pagué veinte dólares [por, para] el libro de texto. (I paid $20 for the textbook.)

6. Viajan a Cuba [por, para] barco. (They're traveling to Cuba by boat.)

7. Mi familia vivió en Puerto Rico [por, para] cinco años. (My family lived in Puerto Rico for 5 years.)

8. Este traje de baño es pequeño [por, para] tí. (This swimsuit is small for you.)

9. Miguel y yo no fuimos a clase ayer [por, para] estar enfermo. (We didn't go to class yesterday because we were sick.)

10. Regresó a su cuarto [por, para] estar enfermo. (He returned to his room because he's sick.)

11. Eses cuadros fueron pintados [por, para] Picasso. (Those paintings were painted by Picasso.)

12. Ese político hace mucho [por, para] los pobres. (That politician does a lot for the poor.)

13. Vamos al centro [por, para] ver una película. (We're going to the center to see a movie.)

14. Quiere viajar [por, para] Europa después de graduarse. (He wants to travel to Europe after graduating.)

15. Si hay un incendio debes salir [por, para] la ventana. (If there's a fire you should leave through the window.)

CAPÍTULO VEINTIDÓS: ¿QUÉ HORA ES? (WHAT TIME IS IT?)

The verb ser is used to express the time of day. Use es when referring to "one o'clock" and use son when referring to all other hours.

Es la una.
It's one o'clock.

Son las dos.
It's two o'clock.

The feminine article (la, las) is used before the hour because it refers to "la hora." "Es la" is used beween 12:31 and 1:30 because it's singular (1). "Son las" is for all other times of the day.

Es la una.
It's one o'clock.

Son las dos.
It's two o'clock.

Minutes can be added to the hour using the word **y** (and).

Es la una y cinco.
It's five minutes past one.

Son las tres y doce.
It's twelve minutes past three.

Minutes can be subtracted from the hour using the word **menos** (less, minus).

Es la una menos cinco.
It's five minutes till one.

Son las tres menos doce.
It's twelve minutes till three.

You can also use the words **media (half) and cuarto (quarter)**.

Es la una y media.
It's half past one.

Son las dos y cuarto.
It's quarter past two.

Son las tres menos cuarto.
It's quarter till three.

To say something occurs at a specific time, use the formula **a + la(s) + time**.

La fiesta empieza a las nueve. (The party begins at nine o'clock.)

El banco abre a las ocho y media. (The bank opens at half past eight.)

To differentiate between a.m. and p.m. use the expressions **de la mañana, de la tarde and de la noche.**

Son las dos de la tarde.
It's two in the afternoon.

Son las dos de la mañana.
It's two in the morning.

Son las diez de la noche.
It's ten in the evening.

When no specific time is mentioned, use the expressions por la mañana, por la tarde, por la noche.

Siempre leo el periódico por las mañanas.
I always read the newspaper in the morning.

Here are a number of useful time expressions:

por la mañana

in the morning (no specific time)

de la mañana

in the morning (specific time)

por la tarde

in the afternoon (no specific time)

de la tarde

in the afternoon (specific time)

por la noche

in the evening or night (no specific time)

de la noche

in the evening or night (specific time)

la mañana

morning

mañana por la mañana

tomorrow morning

pasado mañana

the day after tomorrow

ayer

yesterday

anoche

last night

la noche anterior, anteanoche

the night before last

el lunes que viene

next Monday

la semana que viene

next week

el año que viene

next year

el lunes pasado

last Monday

la semana pasada

last week

el año pasado

last year

al mediodía

at noon

a la medianoche

at midnight

alrededor de

around

durante el día

during the day

a tiempo

on time

en punto

exactly, on-the-dot

tarde

late

temprano

early

PRÁCTICA

Write a sentence to describe the time displayed on each clock. (#1-16)

17. How would you write "at 5:15 in the afternoon?" _____

_____

CAPÍTULO VEINTITRÉS: WEATHER

Describing the Weather in Spanish

In Spanish, certain weather expressions are idiomatic expressions formed with the verb Hacer, some are normal expressions formed by the verb Estar + adjective, and then there are some formed with a single Spanish verb.

¿Cómo está el tiempo? ¿Qué tiempo hace?	How's the weather? What's the weather like?
Está nublado.	It's cloudy.
Está lloviendo.	It's raining.
Está nevando.	It's snowing.
Está húmido.	It's humid.

Hacer

Hacer normally means to do or to make. However, hacer used idiomatically for the weather takes on the meaning: **it is**. Here is a list of idiomatic weather expressions with hacer:

¿Qué tiempo hace?	What's the weather like?
Hace buen tiempo.	It's nice out. (The weather is good).
Hace mal tiempo.	It's bad out. (The weather is bad).
Hace calor.	It's warm.
Hace frío.	It's cold .
Hace viento.	It's windy.
Hace sol.	It's sunny.
Hace fresco.	It's cool.

Note that the literal meaning of these phrases using <u>hace</u> is: It makes + a noun.

So, for example, **hace frío** would literally mean **it makes cold**. However, the translation, or true meaning, is **It's cold**.

Single Verbs

There are, of course, ways to express the weather with specific verbs that will always be conjugated in the 3rd-person singular. For example:

| llover (to rain) | Llueve mucho en Seattle. | It rains a lot in Seattle. |
| nevar (to snow) | Siempre nieva en Nueva York. | It always snows in New York. |

Here are some common ways to ask about the weather:
- ¿Qué tiempo hace?
- ¿Qué clima hace?
- ¿Cómo está el clima en ...?
- ¿Cómo está el tiempo?
- ¿Cómo está el clima hoy?

There are also weather expressions that use the verb hay:
- **Hay niebla.**
  It's foggy.
- **Hay neblina.**
  It's misty.
- **Hay sol.**
  The sun is shining.
- **Hay luna.**
  The moon is out.
- **Hay relámpagos.**
  It's lightning.
- **Hay humedad.**
  It's humid.
- **Hay nubes.**
  It's cloudy.
- **Hay lluvias torrenciales.**
  It's pouring.
- **Hay un vendaval.**
  There's a windstorm.
- **Hay granizo.**
  It's hailing.
- **Hay lloviznas.**
  It's sprinkling.

Other weather expressions use the verb estar along with an adjective:
- **Está oscuro.**
  It's dark.
- **Está nublado.**
  It's cloudy.
- **Está lluvioso.**
  It's raining.

CAPÍTULO VEINTICUATRO: TENER IDIOMS

Tener means "to have". However, in Spanish it takes on many idiomatic expressions that are commonly used.

Conjugating the Present Tense of *Tener*:

Yo	**tengo**	I have
Tú	**tienes**	You have
Usted	**tiene**	You have
Él/Ella	**tiene**	He/She has
Nosotros/as	**tenemos**	We have
Vosotros	**tenéis**	You (all) have
Ustedes	**tienen**	You (all) have
Ellos/Ellas	**tienen**	They have

In Spanish, use the verb *tener*:

1) To express age

¿Cuántos años **tienes**?	How old are you?
Tengo veintidós años.	I am 22 years old

2) To indicate possession

Tengo una casa en California.	I have a house in California.
Tengo cuatro hermanas.	I have four sisters.

3) To indicate obligations

In order to express an obligation, use *tener* + **que** + infinitive

Tengo que estudiar mucho.	I have to study a lot.
¡**Tienes que** prestar atención!	You have to pay attention!

Spanish also has many idiomatic expressions. Although their literal translations sound odd to English speakers, they sound perfectly natural to native speakers. Here is one example:

Idiom: Hace mucho frío

Literally: It makes much cold

True Meaning: It is very cold

There are many idiomatic expressions that use the verb tener. This one expresses age:

Idiom: tener _____ años

Literally: to have _____ years

True Meaning: to be _____ years old

Many other expressions using tener express physical sensations:

tener frío
    to be cold
tener calor
    to be hot
tener hambre
    to be hungry
tener sed
    to be thirsty
tener sueño
    to be sleepy
tener dolor de
    to hurt or be sore, etc.

There are also many idiomatic expressions with tener that express sensations more psychological in nature:

tener prisa
    to be in a hurry
tener miedo a/de + noun
    to be afraid of something
tener miedo a/de + infinitive
    to be afraid to do something
tener celos
    to be jealous
tener confianza
    to be confident
tener cuidado
    to be careful
tener vergüenza
    to be ashamed

There are other idiomatic expressions with tener as well:

tener razón
    to be right
tener éxito
    to be successful
tener la culpa
    to be guilty
tener suerte
    to be lucky
tener lugar
    to take place
tener ganas de
    to feel like
tener en cuenta
    to take into account

When using these idiomatic expressions, conjugate the verb (tener) according to the subject of the sentence.

Yo **tengo** cinco años.
Tú **tienes** ocho años.
Pablo **tiene** dos años.

PRÁCTICA

1. Miguel_____diez años.
Miguel is ten years old.

2. Es un chico muy valiente (brave). No tiene_____a nada.
He is a very brave boy. He's not afraid of anything.

3. Nosotros vamos a la playa porque tengo_____.
We go to the beach because we are hot.

4. Mi madre lleva el abrigo porque_____frío.
My mom wears a coat because she's cold.

5. Voy al restaurante porque tengo mucha_____.
I go to the restaurant because I am very hungry.

6. Bebo agua porque tengo_____.
I drink water because I am thirsty.

7. La clase de español empieza en diez minutos. María necesita tener_____
_____.
The Spanish class starts in ten minutes. Maria needs to hurry.

8. Tengo salud, dinero y amor. Tengo buena_____.
I have health, money and love. I'm lucky.

9. Ellas son muy inteligentes. Ellas siempre_____razón.
They are very intelligent. They are always correct.

10. Muchas personas tienen_____de hablar en público.
Many people are afraid of public speaking.

11. ¿Deseas comer algo? No, no tengo_____.
Do you want to eat something? No, I'm not hungry.

12. ¿Cuántos años tiene María? María_____ diecinueve años.
How old is Maria? Maria is nineteen years old.

13. ¿Por qué llevas el abrigo? Porque_____frío.
Why do you wear the coat? Because I'm cold.

14. ¿Por qué bebes agua? Porque tengo_____.
Why do you drink water? Because I'm thirsty.

15. ¿Por qué comes la carne? Porque tengo_____.
Why do you eat meat? Because I'm hungry.

CAPÍTULO VEINTICINCO: USEFUL SPANISH CONVERSATION WORDS/PHRASES

The following words and phrases are useful to know when having everyday conversation with Spanish speakers.

ESPAÑOL	INGLÉS
Hola	Hello
Buenos días	Good Morning
Buenas tardes	Good Afternoon
Buenas noches	Good Evening
Adiós, hasta luego, ciao	See you later
¿Cómo estás? ¿Cómo está?	How are you? *The first form (which is informal) normally would be used with someone you know on a first-name basis or when speaking with a child. The second form generally would be used in when talking to someone older or to show respect.
bien, muy bien, terrible, horrible, mal, fatal, así-así,	Good, very good, terrible, horrible, bad
Bienvenido, bienvenida, bienvenidos, bienvenidas	Note the difference in number and gender. *Bienvenido* would be used with a man, *bienvenida* with a woman, *bienvenidas* with a group of all females, and *bienvenidos* with males or a mixed group
Hola, aló, jaló, bueno, al, diga	How to answer the phone (depending on location)
¿Cómo te va? ¿Qué tal? ¿Qué hay? ¿Qué pasa? ¿Qué onda?	How's it going? What's happening?

¿Cómo te llamas? (informal) ¿Cómo se llama usted? (Formal)	What is your name?
Me llamo Chris.	My name is Chris. (I call myself Chris.)
Mucho gusto. Encantado/a.	Nice to meet you.
Igualmente	likewise
¿ De dónde eres? (familiar) ¿ De dónde es Ud.? (formal)	Where are you from?
Yo soy de Colombia	I am from Colombia
argentino (a), bolivian(a), chileno (a), domicano(a), estadounidense, mexicano, colombiano(a), costarricense, cubano (a), español, guatemaltec(a), hondureñ(a), mexican(a), nicaragüense, panameñ(a), paraguayo(a), peruan(a), puertorriqueño (a), salvadoreño(a), uruguayo (a), venezolano (a)	If you are from the following countries, these are your nationalities. If the noun is feminine, then the nationality has to agree. Also, the nationalities have to agree in number. Ex. Lisa es mexicana. Lisa y Anita son mexicanas.
¿ Dónde vives?	Where do you live?
Vivo en la ciudad (city).	I live in the city.
¿Cómo eres tú?	Describe yourself. Literally meaning how are you as a person?
Yo soy alto, inteligente, artístico y trabajador.	I am tall, intelligent, artistic and hard working.
¿Cuántos años tienes?	How old are you?
Yo tengo veintiocho años.	I'm 28 years old.
¿Cuándo es tu cumpleaños?	When is your birthday?
Mi cumpleaños es el 6 de mayo.	My birthday is May 6.
¿Qué es tu número de telefóno?	What is your telephone number?

Mi número es……….	My number is…….
¿ Qué tiempo hace?	What is the weather like?
Hace calor, frío, etc.	It's hot, cold, etc.

ANSWER KEYS FOR EACH "PRÁCTICA"

CAPÍTULO 1

No written answers (an oral exercise).

CAPÍTULO 2

1-5: All answers should be lowercase

6-9: All answers should start with "el"

10. martes

11. miércoles

12. jueves

13. viernes

14. sábado

15. domingo

16. lunes

17. marzo, mayo, junio, septiembre, noviembre, enero

18. primer

19. junio

20. cinco

CAPÍTULO 4

1. c
2. a
3. c
4. b
5. d
6. b
7. b
8. c

9. F
10. T
11. F
12. T
13. T
14. F
15. T
16. T
17. unas
18. una
19. una
20. unos

1. a la
2. a la
3. al
4. del
5. de la
6. a la
7. al
8. a las
9. al
10. de la

CAPÍTULO 5

1-10: Words starting with "la" are feminine, "el" are masculine.

11. o
12. a
13. o

14. a

15. o

16. a

17. o

18. a

19. 0

20. a

1. los libros
2. los lápices
3. las universidades
4. las secretarias
5. los mapas
6. las conversaciones

T
F
T
T
T
T
T

-iones

-ces

-as

-es

-es

-s

CAPÍTULO 6

1. esta
2. estas
3. este
4. estas
5. estos
6. esta

1. esa
2. esas
3. esos
4. esa
5. esos
6. eso

1. esas
2. eso
3. esos
4. eso

1. este, eso
2. estos, aquellos
3. esas
4. estas
5. aquellas
6. esta, esa

1. sus amigos
2. su casa
3. nuestros zapatos
4. su restaurante
5. vuestras hermanas
6. mi jugo
7. tu mochila
8. su torta
9. su nariz
10. sus libros y plumas

CAPÍTULO 7

1. qué
2. cómo
3. dónde
4. qué
5. dónde
6. cómo
7. cuándo
8. qué
9. cuántas
10. cómo
11. dónde
12. qué
13. cuántos
14. dónde
15. qué
16. cuándo
17. cómo

18. quién
19. cuál
20. cuántos

CAPÍTULO 8

1. ellas
2. nosotros
3. ellos
4. vosotros
5. ellos
6. él
7. nosotros
8. vosotros
9. nosotros
10. ellos

CAPÍTULO 9

1-12: Answers will vary. Make sure verbs are conjugated for the subjects.

1. C
2. A
3. B
4. A
5. B
6. A
7. C
8. B
9. B
10. A

CAPÍTULO 10

1. soy
2. está
3. somos
4. eres
5. está
6. son
7. está
8. están
9. somos
10. es
11. estamos
12. es
13. estás
14. soy
15. están
16. están
17. está
18. somos

A

1. ser
2. ser
3. ser
4. estar
5. ser
6. estar
7. ser
8. estar
9. ser

B Answers will vary.

1. ser
2. ser
3. estar
4. estar
5. estar
6. estar
7. ser
8. ser
9. ser
10. ser
11. estar
12. estar
13. ser
14. ser
15. estar
16. ser
17. estar
18. estar
19. estar
20. estar

CAPÍTULO 11

1. vienes
2. juegan
3. jugamos
4. comienzan
5. tiene

6. viene
7. tienen
8. prefiere
9. comienzo
10. pierde
11. dormimos
12. vuelve
13. queremos
14. cierra
15. entendemos

CAPÍTULO 12
1. los compramos
2. lo leo
3. la usa
4. la escuchamos
5. los llevo
6. los compré
7. la necesita
8. las veo
9. las busco
10. lo
11. las
12. las
13. lo
14. la
15. nos
16. los
17. te

18. me

19. te

20. te

21. los

22. me

23. te

24. los

25. nos

1. ring

2. her

3. song

4. them

5. bone

6. dog

7. le

8. les

9. me

10. te

CAPÍTULO 13

1. gusta

2. gustan

3. gustan

4. gusta

5. falta

6. falta

7. faltan

8. falta

9. disgusta
10. digustan
11. disgusta
12. disgusta

CAPÍTULO 14

1. se lava
2. nos duchamos
3. se cepillan
4. me afeito
5. se duermen
6. se visten
7. nos sentamos
8. me maquillo

CAPÍTULO 15

1. sabe
2. sé
3. conozco
4. conocen
5. sabe
6. sabe
7. conoce
8. sabe
9. sé

1. pregunto
2. pedir

3. pide
4. preguntar
5. piden
6. pregunta
7. pide

CAPÍTULO 16

1. estamos estudiando
2. estás jugando
3. está escuchando
4. están leyendo
5. estoy montando

1. están mirando
2. estamos preparando
3. están haciendo
4. estás comiendo
5. está escribiendo

CAPÍTULO 17

1. salieron
2. miré
3. escribieron
4. bebimos
5. escuchó
6. comiste
7. llegaron
8. subí
9. perdieron

10. vendió
11. tomamos
12. estudiaron

1. tuvimos
2. vino
3. estuvieron
4. supiste
5. supo
6. fue
7. vieron
8. fue
9. dimos
10. dio

1. estuvieron
2. hicimos
3. pudiste
4. quise
5. puso
6. hizo

(For the sentence activity, answers will vary.)

1. estudiaban
2. llamaba
3. llamaba
4. estaba
5. estaba

6. comíamos
7. eran
8. estabas
9. llamaba
10. limpiaba
11. podías
12. escribían
13. estaba
14. estudiaba
15. vivían
16. veías
17. veían
18. estaban
19. iba
20. iba

CAPÍTULO 18

1. tendremos
2. saldrán
3. Irán
4. dirás
5. podrán
6. haré
7. querrá
8. se despertarán
9. sabrán
10. me levantaré
11. pondrá
12. dirá

13. iré
14. asistiremos
15. seré
16. estarás
17. prepararán
18. sacará

1. compraría
2. comería
3. esquiarían
4. llevarían
5. saldría
6. haríamos
7. irías
8. podrían
9. diría
10. pondría
11. iríais
12. sería
13. visitaría
14. querrían

CAPÍTULO 19

1. has vivido
2. he comido
3. hemos estudiado
4. habéis visto

5. han hablado
6. han salido
7. han sido/estado
8. he bebido
9. hemos escuchado
10. ha lavado

1. había
2. hablado
3. había
4. jugado
5. habías
6. volado
7. habían
8. cocinado
9. había
10. hablado
11. había
12. habíamos

CAPÍTULO 20
1. por
2. para
3. para
4. por
5. por
6. por
7. por
8. para

9. por
10. por
11. por
12. para
13. para
14. para
15. por

CAPÍTULO 22
1. Son las dos.
2. Son las doce.
3. Son las seis.
4. Son las seis y media/treinta.
5. Son las nueve y veinticinco.
6. Son las seis y once.
7. Son las dos y veinticuatro.
8. Son las cuatro menos cinco.
9. Son las cinco menos diez.
10. Son las nueve y veintiuno.
11. Son las cinco y cuatro.
12. Son las diez y veinticuatro.
13. Son las doce y cinco.
14. Son las once menos veintiuno.
15. Son las diez y veinticinco.
16. Son las dos menos cuarto/quince.
17. A las cinco y cuarto/quince de la tarde.

CAPÍTULO 24

1. tiene
2. miedo
3. calor
4. tiene
5. hambre
6. sed
7. prisa
8. suerte
9. tienen
10. miedo
11. hambre
12. tiene
13. tengo
14. sed
15. hambre